# Bristol & Bath
# Hidden Walks

Michael Wilberforce

Published by Geographers'
A-Z Map Company Limited
An imprint of HarperCollins Publishers
Westerhill Road
Bishopbriggs
Glasgow
G64 2QT

HarperCollinsPublishers
1st Floor, Watermarque Building,
Ringsend Road, Dublin 4, Ireland

www.az.co.uk
a-z.maps@harpercollins.co.uk

1st edition 2022

ISBN 978-0-00-849635-7

10 9 8 7 6 5 4 3 2 1

Printed in the UK

**MIX**
Paper from
responsible sources
**FSC™ C007454**

# contents

# introduction

On the face of it, the two neighbouring cities of Bristol and Bath have little in common: one is a cosmopolitan maritime city with a robust industrial heritage, and the other is a small, picturesque Georgian spa city with Roman roots. Bath is a magnet for mainstream tourism, while tourism in Bristol is built more around its thriving cultural scene including its live music and street art.

However, dig a little deeper and you will find both cities have a shared heritage. Both cities were built around the River Avon and its valleys and are intimately connected by road, rail and water. Both cities are rich with built and natural heritage. Both cities have hot springs whose waters were once taken by wealthy people in poor health, hoping for a miracle cure. Both cities feature steep hills and panoramic views, and both cities have unique green spaces and secluded places where, even today, the urban meets the wild.

The walks in this book seek to get under the skin of both cities, looking beyond the obvious tourist attractions to discover the hidden streams, gardens, valleys and squares that define the urban landscape. They take to the hills in search of the best views, finding hidden paths and flights of steps away from the bustle of urban traffic, and they visit old rural villages absorbed by the creeping spread of the city. In this book, even lifelong residents will find somewhere new to discover and explore.

## about the author

Michael Wilberforce has been a professional town planner for over 15 years. He is a keen walker who has been exploring the streets and spaces of his home city of Bristol since childhood. His previous work on urban walks has helped Bristolians to explore and discover the hidden delights of their own local area.

# how to use this book

Each of the 20 walks in this guide is set out in a similar way. They are all introduced with a brief description, including notes on things you will encounter on your walk, and a photograph of a place of interest you might pass along the way.

On the first page of each walk there is a panel of information outlining the distance of the walk, a guide to the walking time, and a brief description of the path conditions

or the terrain you will encounter. A suggested starting point along with the nearest postcode is shown, although postcodes can cover a large area therefore this is just a rough guide.

The major part of each section is taken up with route maps and detailed point-to-point directions for the walk. The route instructions are prefixed by a number in a circle, and the corresponding location is shown on the map.

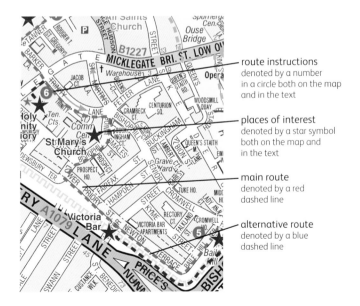

**route instructions**
denoted by a number in a circle both on the map and in the text

**places of interest**
denoted by a star symbol both on the map and in the text

**main route**
denoted by a red dashed line

**alternative route**
denoted by a blue dashed line

# ᴀZ walk one

# The Old City

Secrets of medieval Bristol.

Most visitors to Bristol are likely to take in the popular attractions such as the Clifton Suspension Bridge, Brunel's SS Great Britain, and Floating Harbour. But they may miss the city's many ancient churches and surviving medieval thoroughfares. This walk explores those features that are hidden in plain sight in the heart of the city centre.

The walk starts on the Centre Promenade for a glimpse of the city's iconic Floating Harbour, an impressive feat of early 19th-century engineering that turned a tidal river into a harbour with a fixed water level. The Centre Promenade, which hosts a lively street food market at weekends, is also where you will find the Hippodrome theatre and Bristol Beacon concert hall.

As you explore the Old City, look out for its many surviving medieval churches, some of which are open to visitors, and the handsome former Corn Exchange. You will get to visit the vibrant surrounds of St Nicholas Markets and historic King Street, which features buildings from almost every architectural era. After experiencing the Georgian splendour of Queen Square, you will pass through the city's regenerated Harbourside area to reach Bristol Cathedral.

An optional extension to the route climbs Park Street, passing several historic museums and monuments and returning to the Centre Promenade via the atmospheric confines of Christmas Steps.

| | |
|---|---|
| start / finish | The Centre Promenade, Bristol |
| nearest postcode | BS1 4UZ |
| distance | 1½ miles / 2.3 km (+ optional ¾ mile / 1.1 km) |
| time | 1 hour (+ optional 30 minutes) |
| terrain | All surfaced roads and paths, some steps. The optional extension includes one major climb. |

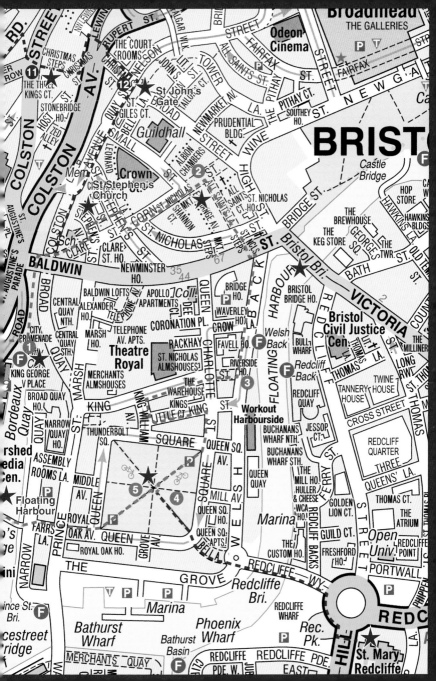

Park in either of the Trenchard Street or College Street car parks; or take the short walk to the Centre Promenade from Bristol Temple Meads Station (15 minutes) or any city centre bus stop.

**1** Start by making your way up the Centre Promenade ★ from the water's edge until you reach Baldwin Street. Cross Baldwin Street and bear right along pedestrianized Clare Street. Take a detour via the first left and a parallel footpath to see St Stephen's Church ★ with its delicate tower. Return to Clare Street as it becomes Corn Street, entering the original walled medieval city, later the city's banking district.

**2** At the top of the hill, you will reach the former Corn Exchange, which is one of the entrances to the vibrant St Nicholas Markets ★. Just past the Corn Exchange, turn right into narrow, ancient All Saints Lane and make your way down through the markets, then carry on down a flight of stone steps to return to Baldwin Street. Cross Baldwin Street and go roughly straight on along Welsh Back for a view of the Floating Harbour and historic Bristol Bridge ★.

**3** Just before buildings enclose both sides of the street, turn right into picturesque, cobbled King Street. You will pass the Bristol Old Vic theatre, whose modern lobby/bar area contains a fragment of the old city wall. Turn left along King William Avenue and double back along Little King Street to the rear, reaching Queen Charlotte Street outside The Granary, a striking building built in 1869 in the distinctive 'Bristol Byzantine' style. Turn right and head to the centre of the grand, tree-lined Queen Square ★.

**4** You have the option to take a detour from here to visit St Mary Redcliffe ★, Bristol's finest parish church, on the other side of the Floating Harbour. To do this, leave Queen Square via Bell Avenue at the far left-hand corner. Go straight on across Redcliffe Bascule Bridge and bear right past the large roundabout. Cross Redcliff Hill. The church is best approached from its peaceful rear churchyard. Retrace your steps to Queen Square when you have finished.

**5** Exit the square via Royal Oak Avenue, diagonally opposite the corner at which you first arrived. Go straight across Prince Street to approach the Floating Harbour via Farrs Lane. Cross Pero's Bridge to reach Anchor Square ★, part of the city's lively regenerated Harbourside area.

**6** Exit Anchor Square via the far right-hand corner and cross busy Anchor Road. Climb the stone steps ahead of you to reach College Green ★ , home to Bristol Cathedral ★ and City Hall. Take a walk around the green for a closer look at the cathedral, the historic Norman Arch ★ next to it and the Central Library ★ . The cathedral is worth a visit for its spacious interior and peaceful churchyard.

**Optional additional walk**

**8** From College Green, climb historic Park Street. About halfway up, pay a visit to Great George Street (off left) to see the beautiful St George's concert hall ★ and the tucked-away Georgian House Museum ★ and continue straight on, all the way back, an authentically preserved Georgian merchant's house. Retrace your steps to Park Street and continue your climb.

**9** At the top of the hill you will find the University of Bristol's imposing Wills Memorial Building ★ and the Bristol City Museum and Art Gallery ★ . Optionally, take a detour into Berkeley Square to find the remains of Bristol's Georgian High Cross ★ , which once stood on College Green. Its medieval predecessor can now be found on the National Trust's Stourhead estate in Wiltshire. Retrace your steps along Berkeley Avenue.

**10** From the top of Park Street, turn right to follow busy Park Row. Here you will find the Red Lodge Museum ★ ,

**7** From College Green, you have the option to return to the start on the Centre Promenade by heading back down the main road (to the right as you stand with your back to the cathedral). Alternatively, you can follow the extension described below to explore more of the city's history.

a partially furnished Elizabethan house with a remarkable moulded ceiling. Opposite, watch out for the city synagogue ★ , recognizable by the Hebrew writing above the entrance. After a while, Park Row becomes Perry Road. Turn right down a flight of steep stone steps opposite the shops for a view of the city's skyline.

**11** Cross Colston Street and continue down the quaint, atmospheric medieval thoroughfare of Christmas Steps ★ . Bear left past a row of ancient timber-framed buildings and walk beneath a modern office building to reach an open area on Lewins Mead. Cross the main road and cut through Christmas Street, opposite the bottom of Christmas Steps, to reach St John's Gate, the largest surviving fragment of the original city wall.

**12** Finally, turn right along Quay Street and continue straight on, all the way back to the Centre Promenade.

# ᴀᴢ walk two

## Survivors of the Blitz

Two centuries of development north of the centre.

The northern edge of Bristol City Centre is defined by a steep escarpment running from Kingsdown in the east to Clifton in the west. The hillside underwent a great deal of development during the Georgian period as wealthy merchants sought to relocate out of the increasingly crowded central area.

The legacy of this period was a series of attractive Georgian terraces and squares bordering the city centre. Some have survived, while others were lost to the Blitz of 1940–1 and the subsequent postwar development, resulting in a slightly fragmented feel.

This challenging and hilly walk ties the surviving Georgian development together into a single route and explores some of the quirky and interesting hinterland spaces where the expansion of the hospital and university precincts has impinged on older residential areas away from the usual tourist trail.

Starting from the Centre Promenade, you will visit some medieval thoroughfares before passing through the city centre's main shopping area. From there, you will visit the Georgian squares of St Paul's before climbing up to the heights of Kingsdown with its panoramic city views. Making your way up and down the escarpment, you will explore a maze of hidden lanes around St Michael's Hill before visiting two major green spaces at the top of the hill, passing through the lively Clifton Triangle along the way.

| | |
|---|---|
| **start / finish** | The Centre Promenade, Bristol |
| **nearest postcode** | BS1 4UZ |
| **distance** | 5 miles / 8 km |
| **time** | 3 hours 30 minutes |
| **terrain** | All surfaced roads and paths, steeply hilly with some steps. |

Park in either of the Trenchard Street or College Street car parks; or take the short walk to the Centre Promenade from Bristol Temple Meads Station (15 minutes) or any city centre bus stop.

**1** From the Centre Promenade ★, walk uphill from the water's edge and cross the main road to your left. Bear left to pass Bristol Beacon concert hall ★ at the bottom of Colston Street. Bear right into Host Street. At the bottom of the hill, turn right into a covered walkway. Bear left past medieval Christmas Steps, and then continue through the next covered walkway to reach Lewins Mead.

**2** Take the tiny turning on the left, Johnny Ball Lane. At the top of the hill, turn right into Upper Maudlin Street. Take the first right into Lower Maudlin Street. St James' Priory ★, at the bottom of Whitson Street, is the oldest building in Bristol.

**3** Take the short flight of steps just after The White Hart to reach St James' Churchyard. Turn right down a tree-lined walkway and cross the main road. Go straight on into Union Street.

**4** Turn left into the Broadmead shopping precinct. Historic survivors include a Victorian shopping arcade and John Wesley's New Room ★, the oldest Methodist building in the world. Continue along George White Street to enter the Cabot Circus shopping centre with its striking glass roof.

**5** Staying on the middle level of the shopping centre, bear left and exit via Stratton Lane. Emerging on Bond Street, go straight across to reach Pritchard Street. Turn right into Norfolk Avenue, left into St Paul Street and then right into Wilson Street. Turn left into Lemon Lane to reach St Paul's Park.

**6** Take the narrow footway to the left of the church. Cross grand Portland Square and take Surrey Street opposite to reach historic Brunswick Square.

**7** Leave Brunswick Square via Upper York Street, bearing left at the end to reach Stokes Croft, with its independent spirit. Cross Stokes Croft and turn left.

**8** Take the next right to approach King Square, a Georgian survivor. Cross the square and climb steeply up Spring Hill until you reach a crossroads with the delightful, cobbled Somerset Street. Check out the view behind you, then turn right and follow Somerset Street to the far end.

**9** Take a loop around quiet Fremantle Square. Double back towards Kingsdown Parade and take the first right into Fremantle Road. Turn left into Cotham Side to reach St Matthew's Church. Take the first left into St Matthew's Road and follow it to a crossroads. Optionally, take a hard left and explore Back of Kingsdown Parade, an atmospheric mews lit by gas lamps. Return to the crossroads.

**10** Turn left into Clevedon Terrace and, at the end, left into Kingsdown Parade. Take the first right and descend Montague Hill until you reach a footpath above Dove Street. Turn right into Marlborough Hill Place.

**11** Reaching a crossroads, turn right up Marlborough Hill and then left into an NHS car park. Walk through the car park and cross Alfred Hill to reach a woodland walk through the hospital. Emerging on Horfield Road opposite Bengough's Almshouses, turn left and walk down to the junction of St Michael's Hill and Perry Road.

**12** Cross St Michael's Hill at the traffic lights, climb back up slightly and immediately turn left into Lower Church Lane. Take the steps on the right to approach St Michael's Church, then make an anticlockwise loop around the church to reach Upper Church Lane. At the end of the lane, turn right up Old Park Hill, passing a row of quirky cottages below the university precinct. Turn right into Old Park, left into Park Lane, climbing a few steps, and right into Park Place to return to St Michael's Hill opposite Colston's Almshouses.

**13** Climb St Michael's Hill, negotiating a few more steps. Turn left up Royal Fort Road to enter Bristol University's Royal Fort Gardens ★ via an historic gatehouse. Turn left past Royal Fort House to make a clockwise circuit of the gardens, eventually emerging on Woodland Road.

**14** Cross Woodland Road and descend Elton Road past Bristol Grammar School. Continue straight on at the end to reach Queen's Road.

**15** Turn left into Queen's Road. At the far end of the Clifton Triangle shops ★ , cross Queen's Road at the traffic lights and make the short climb into the Georgian Berkeley Square.

**16** Leave Berkeley Square via the far corner, then take the first left to enter Brandon Hill park. Turn right and climb the winding paths to Cabot Tower ★ at the top of the hill. Explore the park as you make your way down the far side to reach the bottom left-hand corner, passing the end of Great George Street on the way.

**17** Emerging at the top of Brandon Steep, go straight on down a narrow footpath called Brandon Steps. Turn left onto St George's Road and then cross over, passing through a pocket park to the rear of City Hall. Turn left onto College Street and then right into Frog Lane.

**18** Passing under Park Street, bear right in front of the ancient Hatchet pub. Turn right into Denmark Avenue, which becomes Denmark Street. When you reach the junction with Gaunt's Lane, turn left to return to the Centre Promenade via the pleasant Augustine's Courtyard. If the gates are shut, return via Denmark Street.

# **A̅Z walk three**

## **The Clifton Hillside**

Secret lanes, hidden gardens and quiet terraces in
Clifton Wood and Hotwells.

Fashionable Clifton is firmly on the tourist trail, and so are the nearby City
Docks. Less well known, however, is the steep hillside area that separates the
two, covering the residential communities of Clifton Wood and Hotwells.
The hillside is criss-crossed with many fascinating lanes, steep flights of steps
and hidden gardens. This walk takes you on a secret journey through the
best of them.

Starting at the Centre Promenade, you will make your way through the
city's regenerated Harbourside area until you reach White Hart Steps, the
first of the many hidden paths and lanes that feature on this walk.

Climbing steeply up the hillside, you will arrive among the Victorian villas
of Clifton Wood. Reaching Clifton itself you will then plunge back down to
Hotwells to discover the secluded delights of the Polygon, a hidden Georgian
crescent with a wonderfully peaceful garden.

After a brief detour to see the view-commanding Georgian terraces at
Windsor Terrace and the Paragon, you will walk along a section of the
dramatic Avon Gorge before climbing the challenging Zig-Zag path back up
to Clifton. Passing briefly through the heart of Clifton Village, you will make
your way back down through the unassuming Victorian terraces of Clifton
Wood before skirting Brandon Hill and Bristol Cathedral on your way back to
the Centre Promenade.

| | |
|---|---|
| **start / finish** | The Centre Promenade, Bristol |
| **nearest postcode** | BS1 4UZ |
| **distance** | 4 miles / 6.2 km |
| **time** | 2 hours 15 minutes |
| **terrain** | All surfaced roads and paths, steeply hilly with steps. |

Park in either of the Trenchard Street or College Street car parks; or take the short walk to the Centre Promenade from Bristol Temple Meads Station (15 minutes) or any city centre bus stop.

**1** From the Centre Promenade ★, start by walking along Bordeaux Quay, on the right-hand side of the Floating Harbour ★. Turn right at Pero's Bridge to enter Anchor Square. Keep to the left as you pass through Anchor Square so that you enter Millennium Square.

**2** Cross the top of Millennium Square and head for the Millennium Promenade on the far side. Follow the promenade until you descend to a harbour inlet at the water's edge. Turn right, skirt the inlet and climb the steps on the far side, then turn right into Gasworks Lane.

**3** At the end of the lane, turn left to follow Anchor Road until you reach the Jacob's Wells Roundabout. Make your way around the roundabout in an anticlockwise direction, crossing St George's Road and Jacob's Wells Road. Step through a tunnel under St Peter's House, a large block of flats, to access White Hart Steps. Climb the atmospheric steps, passing isolated houses and charming secluded gardens.

**4** At the top of the steps, bear left onto Worlds End Lane to reach Southernhay. Bear right up the ramp leading to Clifton Wood Road. Follow the road to the far end then turn left up Constitution Hill to reach Clifton. Turn left and follow Lower Clifton Hill towards Clifton Village. Cross the top of Goldney Avenue to continue through a green area.

**5** Just before the shops, turn left down Hensman's Hill to approach the faded grandeur of Cornwallis Crescent. Turn right onto Cornwallis Crescent and then cross the road. Take Polygon Lane, the narrow footpath next to the first lamppost on the left. After a short and winding descent into Hotwells you will see The Polygon ★ itself, an attractive Georgian crescent nestling in a tucked-away location at the foot of the hill, at the heart of a maze of quiet lanes and cul-de-sacs.

**6** Continue straight on past the garden to reach Hopechapel Hill. Turn right and climb the hill. Reaching Granby Hill, turn right and then immediately left up Victoria Terrace to see Windsor Terrace and the Paragon and admire the view. Retrace your steps to Granby Hill. Turn right and then immediately right again into Hinton Lane.

**7** Descend to Hotwell Road and turn right to walk along the Avon Gorge ★ for a while. Eventually you will pass a stone facade set into the rockface, propped up with concrete buttresses: this is the lower entrance to the defunct Clifton Rocks Railway, a funicular which provided train services between Hotwells and Clifton via a tunnel running steeply up through the cliff.

**8** The pavement ends at a flight of steps. Climb the steps to make the steep ascent to Clifton via the winding Zig-Zag path, with views of the Clifton Suspension Bridge ★ . Turn right and make your way down Sion Hill, passing the top station of the Clifton Rocks Railway.

**9** Take the second left, Princess Victoria Street, and follow it to the far end, entering the heart of Clifton Village. Turn right onto Clifton Down Road, which shortly becomes Regent Street, and retrace your steps to Goldney Avenue.

**10** Turn right onto Goldney Avenue and then left onto Goldney Lane, a narrow little footpath running down the hill just below Goldney Hall. At the bottom of the path, turn left along Ambra Vale East. Passing Cliftonwood Community Garden, you will soon reach a crossroads with Church Lane.

**11** Go straight on into Cliftonwood Crescent to return to Southernhay. Turn right into Southernhay Avenue and follow the little footpath at the far end to return to Worlds End Lane. Turn right and then make your way back down White Hart Steps.

**12** Cross the bottom of Jacob's Wells Road and begin to climb. Take the steep little staircase on the right to reach a footpath at the bottom of Brandon Hill. Turn right to approach Queen's Parade.

**13** When you reach the houses, turn right into York Place. Turn left into St George's Road and go straight on along Deanery Road to reach College Green. Continue past Bristol Cathedral ★ and follow the main road to return to the Centre Promenade.

# **A̶Z** walk four

## Fashionable Clifton

Hidden corners behind the famous sights.

No visit to Bristol is complete without a trip to this desirable neighbourhood, where the iconic Clifton Suspension Bridge spans the dramatic Avon Gorge. Nearby Clifton Village has all the buzz of a vibrant market town, with boutique shops and plenty of places to eat and drink. The finest of Clifton's residential terraces and crescents are easily the equal of Georgian Bath. However, within a short walk of these famous sights, there are also many interesting little corners and features to be found.

Starting from The Promenade at Clifton Down, a grand avenue of beech trees, you will climb up to Observatory Hill, where you can take photographs of the Clifton Suspension Bridge or visit the Giant's Cave or camera obscura at the Observatory; children will be bound to want to try the famous rock slide.

Having seen the major sights, you will descend gently to the spectacular, view-commanding Royal York Crescent before making your way to the peaceful oasis of St Andrew's Churchyard. After a walk through the buzzing heart of Clifton Village you will retreat to a network of quiet back streets full of unique mews houses, including the unexpected delight of the triangular Canynge Square.

| | |
|---|---|
| **start / finish** | The Promenade, at the junction of Bridge Valley Road and Clifton Down, Bristol |
| **nearest postcode** | BS8 3HT |
| **distance** | 2½ miles / 4 km |
| **time** | 1 hour 30 minutes |
| **terrain** | All surfaced roads and paths, some steps. |

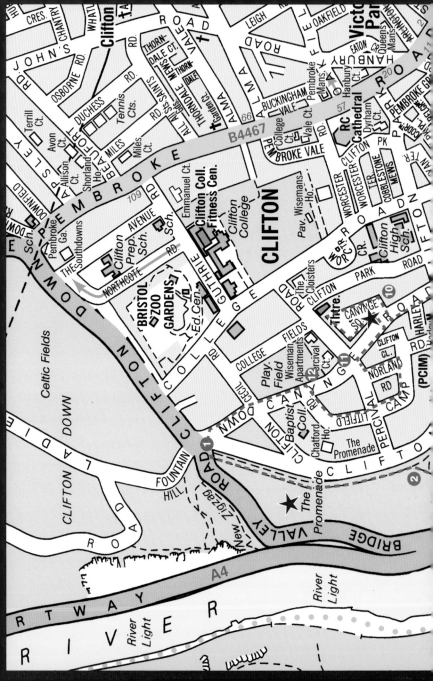

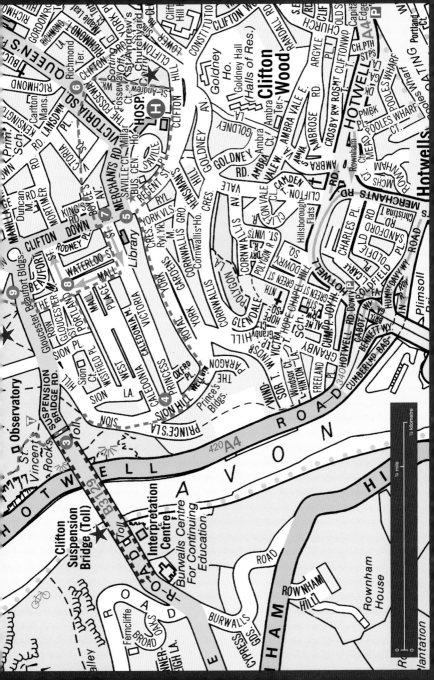

On-street parking is available close to the start point along Clifton Down, The Promenade or Percival Road (charges apply); or take the bus to the 'Bristol Zoo' bus stop on Clifton Down, close to the junction with College Road (note that due to the relocation of the zoo in late 2022, this bus stop name may be altered).

**1** Starting at the top of Bridge Valley Road, begin the walk by heading along the grand avenue of beech trees at The Promenade ★, keeping to the right-hand side of the road and climbing gently until you reach a fork in the path, level with the grand-looking Engineers' House on the other side of the road.

**2** Take the right fork and climb to Observatory Hill. Follow the clifftop path for great views of the Clifton Suspension Bridge ★. As you begin to descend again, you will pass the top of a rocky slope which has been polished over the centuries by the bottoms of all the local children who have used it as a slide. Take a hard right down a footpath that leads past the bottom of the rock slide, coming out on Suspension Bridge Road.

**3** You have the option here to take a walk across the bridge and back. Otherwise, cross Suspension Bridge Road and take the footpath opposite, crossing Christchurch Green. Turn right down Sion Hill. At the corner of Prince's Lane you will find the top station of the defunct Clifton Rocks Railway, a funicular which provided train services between Clifton and Hotwells via a tunnel running steeply down through the cliff.

**4** At the junction with Princess Victoria Street, take the raised pavement along Wellington Terrace. Just before the next junction, climb the steep steps on the left to reach the raised pedestrian promenade of Royal York Crescent. Enjoy the view as you follow it.

**5** Turn right into Regent Street. When the road splits, take the left fork, Clifton Hill. Go through the iron gates on the left to reach St Andrew's Churchyard ★. Follow the walkway through the middle.

**6** Coming out at a complex junction, cross Queen's Road and take the footpath that runs diagonally across the centre of Victoria Square. At the far corner, step through a stone archway to reach Boyce's Avenue next to the tucked-away Clifton Arcade.

**7** Turn left onto Clifton Down Road and then immediately right into Princess Victoria Street to enter the heart of Clifton Village. Take the second right, The Mall, passing Caledonia Place and West Mall with their lovely central gardens.

**8** You will reach a crossroads with Portland Street. Take a brief detour to the left to see three very Dickensian-looking residential courtyards, a very little-known corner of Clifton. Return to the crossroads and continue up The Mall towards Christchurch Green ★ .

**9** Cross Suspension Bridge Road at the zebra crossing and take the footpath, second from right, that crosses the green heading slightly to the right. Make your way across the green, crossing two roads, to reach quiet Canynge Road.

**10** Take the first right off Canynge Road to explore Canynge Square ★ , a peaceful close framed by handsome houses and lit by gas lamps. Return to Canynge Road and continue until you reach a crossroads.

**11** Turn left onto Percival Road and left again onto Norland Road. Emerging on Camp Road, follow it round to the right past a row of interesting mews houses. Go straight on into Litfield Road.

**12** Litfield Road brings you back out on Canynge Road. Turn left to pass the Mansion House, the official residence of the Lord Mayor of Bristol, as you come back out on Clifton Down. Go straight on to return to the end of the Promenade.

# ᴀz walk five

## South of the River

Bedminster, Totterdown and Arno's Vale.

The inner part of southeast Bristol has one of highest concentrations of unique and natural green spaces in the city, among them the partially restored wilderness of Arno's Vale Cemetery.

Starting on the River Avon at Bedminster Bridge, you will glimpse one of the former tobacco factories that once formed the beating heart of the industrial suburb of Bedminster. Heading east, you will encounter the secluded charm of Windmill Hill City Farm before visiting the rolling and spacious Victoria Park, which is one of Bristol's largest formal green spaces.

Climbing up to the Edwardian suburb of Knowle via Perrett Park, which offers some of the best long-distance views in the city, you will go on to discover the wonderful lost landscape of Arno's Vale Cemetery. The Victorian garden cemetery, which includes several listed monuments and two restored chapels, was neglected for many years and parts of it are now a wooded wilderness and a haven for wildlife.

After a detour via the modern riverside Paintworks community, you will climb back up to tour the iconic colourful terraced streets of Totterdown on your way back to Bedminster.

Note that the gates to Arno's Vale Cemetery may be closed in the evening.

| | |
|---|---|
| start / finish | Bedminster Bridge Roundabout, Bristol |
| nearest postcode | BS3 4JA |
| distance | 4½ miles / 7.4 km |
| time | 2 hours 30 minutes |
| terrain | Surfaced roads and paths, with optional unsurfaced sections. Steep hills and three long flights of steps. |

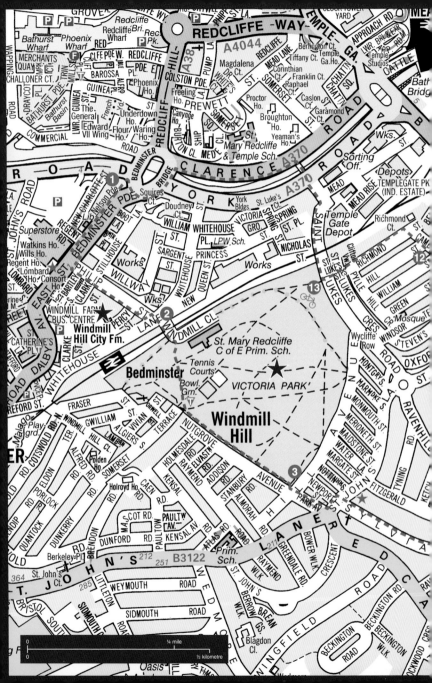

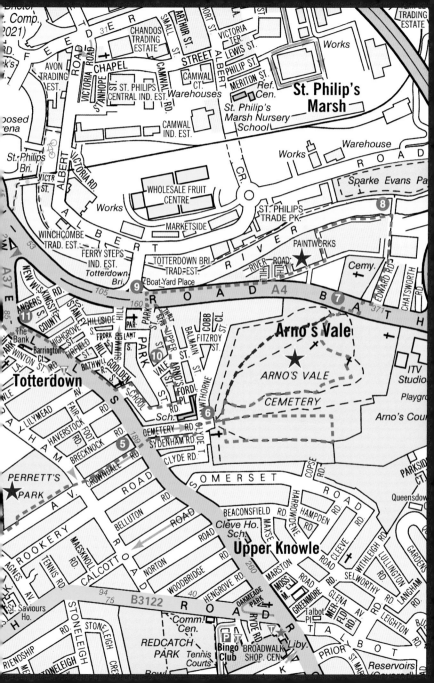

Park in the Bedminster Parade public car park next to Bedminster Bridge Roundabout; or take the short walk from Bristol Temple Meads Station (15 minutes) or a bus to Bedminster Parade.

**1** From Bedminster Bridge Roundabout, walk south along Bedminster Parade/Nelson Parade towards East Street. The former tobacco factory lies ahead of you. Turn left opposite the supermarket onto Philip Street. You will pass the tucked-away Windmill Hill City Farm ★ , which has been delighting and educating young Bristolians for decades.

**2** At the end of the road, go through the tunnel under the railway tracks opposite to reach the foot of Victoria Park ★ . Go straight on up the steps to reach the rose garden. Passing the park lodge, follow the avenue of lime trees along the right-hand edge of the park next to Nutgrove Avenue.

**3** At the bottom of the hill, go straight on into Park Avenue. Turn left onto St John's Lane until you have passed the mini-roundabout, then cross over and climb the next residential street, Sylvia Avenue.

**4** At the junction at the top of the hill, continue straight on into the next section of Sylvia Avenue. Go through the park gate on the left and follow the path along the top of Perrett's Park ★ , which offers panoramic views over Clifton, south Bristol and the North Somerset countryside. An interpretation plaque identifies various city landmarks. Leave the park via the corner gate and go straight on into Crowndale Road.

**5** Reaching busy Wells Road next to Totterdown Baptist Church, go straight across into Sydenham Road, which has colourful terraced houses typical of Totterdown. Turn left onto Clyde Terrace and then right onto Cemetery Road to approach the upper gates of Arno's Vale Cemetery ★ .

**6** Explore the cemetery at your leisure. A suggested route starts with an anticlockwise loop of the upper, meadow-like area, turning left at the war memorial to head back towards the top gates; followed by a wander down through the wilderness of self-seeded trees at the heart of the cemetery, which you can access via a track off the main driveway at 'Sunshine Corner'. Alternatively, to avoid short unsurfaced sections, head straight down the main driveway. When you've finished, leave the cemetery via the main gates onto Bath Road.

**7** Turn right onto Bath Road, cross over at the traffic lights and then turn left down Edward Road. At the end, continue along a footpath.

**8** Just before you reach a yellow suspension bridge across the river, turn left into Paintworks ★, a modern community developed on the site of a former Victorian paint factory. Follow the main access road through Paintworks, turning left and then right. Returning to Bath Road, continue straight on until you reach the traffic lights.

**9** Cross Bath Road at the traffic lights. Double back briefly and then turn right up steep Thunderbolt Steps. It's quite a long climb, so take it gently. You will come out on Upper Street, Totterdown, where the terraced houses genuinely look like they are about to 'totter down' the hill.

**10** At the top of the hill you will reach a crossroads. Off right, Vale Street is said to be the steepest residential street in England. Go straight across into Arno's Street, following it round the corner into School Road. You will eventually emerge on Wells Road next to Holy Nativity Church with its distinctive tower of red brick and green copper. Turn right and head downhill.

**11** At a busy junction with traffic lights, cross Wells Road and the end of St John's Lane then cut through to the left of the local supermarket on the corner to reach Oxford Street. Turn right along Oxford Street, immediately left into Cheapside Street past The Oxford pub, then right again into Henry Street. The side turnings to the left offer views towards Victoria Park.

**12** At the end of the road, turn right onto William Street and then immediately left onto Cambridge Street, climbing to the top of the hill. Turn left onto Richmond Street. Continue straight on to descend steep St Luke's Steps, noting the tucked-away terrace of Clifton View on the right.

**13** Reaching St Lukes Road opposite Victoria Park, turn right and follow the road under the railway lines. When you come out on York Road, go straight on across the Langton Street Bridge, known locally as the Banana Bridge, to reach Clarence Road. Turn left along Clarence Road, following the River Avon New Cut, to return to Bedminster Bridge.

# Az walk six

## The Secret Slopes

Hills, views and greenery in the southern suburbs.

The suburban streets of south Bristol are not known for their picturesque quality; however, dig a little deeper and you can find several unique green spaces, some of which have tremendous city views. This circuit explores several of these places, spending more of its time in green surroundings than it does on city streets.

Starting outside Holy Nativity Church, Totterdown, a local landmark whose distinctive green copper tower can be seen for miles around, the route proceeds straight to Perrett's Park, Knowle, where the views stretch all the way out to Clifton and the North Somerset countryside. Descending from Knowle, the walk crosses through the heart of Victoria Park, one of Bristol's largest Victorian green spaces, to reach Windmill Hill. From there, the route picks up the Malago Greenway, following south Bristol's little-known main river through a series of green spaces until you reach the foot of Nover's Hill.

Climbing the steep Nover's Steps, the route reaches the Northern Slopes: a series of semi-wild green areas on the undeveloped hillside between Bedminster and Knowle. Each of the three separate Northern Slopes areas you will visit has something different to offer; with plentiful wildlife interest and spectacular city views to be had, the slopes are probably south Bristol's best kept secret.

| | |
|---|---|
| **start / finish** | Holy Nativity Church, Wells Road, Totterdown, Bristol |
| **nearest postcode** | BS4 2AG |
| **distance** | 4¼ miles / 6.9 km |
| **time** | 2 hours 15 minutes |
| **terrain** | A mix of surfaced and unsurfaced paths and roads; parts may be slippery in winter. Steep hills and one long flight of steps. |

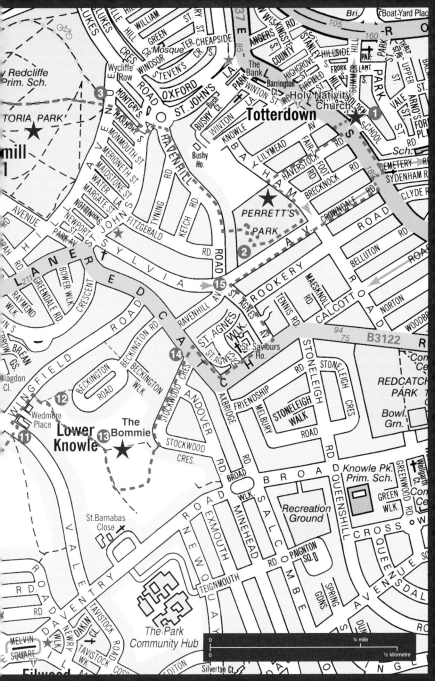

Park on School Road or among the residential streets on the other side of Wells Road; or take the bus to Wells Road, Totterdown (bus stop 'Brecknock Road').

**1** Starting outside Holy Nativity Church ★ , cross Wells Road and take Haverstock Road opposite to reach Bayham Road. Turn left and then enter Perrett's Park ★ at the first gate. Follow the footpath around the top of the park until you reach the top of another tarmac footpath that zig-zags down the hill.

**2** Turn down the footpath and leave the park via the gate next to the playground, emerging on Ravenhill Road. Turn right and go downhill. At the roundabout, turn left onto St John's Lane, cross at the zebra crossing and then take the next right, Marmaduke Street, to reach Victoria Park ★ .

**3** Enter the park and go straight on to climb the hill. Continue up an avenue of mature lime trees.

**4** Crest the hill with the tennis courts on your left. Looking to the left after the tennis courts you will see a three-way fork. Take the middle fork to reach the rose garden. Go straight on and descend along the edge of the park, leaving via the gate onto Fraser Street.

**5** Descend Fraser Street, reaching a crossroads with Windmill Hill at the entrance to Bedminster Station. Cross Windmill Hill to Cotswold Road North. Immediately turn right onto the Malago Greenway cycle path, descending past an open green area. Follow the River Malago until you come back out on St John's Lane.

**6** Cross St John's Lane at the traffic lights and take Francis Road opposite. Quickly reaching Bedminster Road, cross over and take the footpath opposite, keeping the river to your left. Cross a footbridge to return to the main Malago Greenway. Carry on through Marksbury Road Open Space ★ .

**7** Turn right onto Marksbury Road until you reach a small stone bridge over the river. Turn left just before the bridge to continue along the Malago Greenway. Keeping the river to your right, you will pass through another area of greenery.

**8** Leave via the gates onto Parson Street and turn left. At the next junction, take the footpath that climbs up towards steep steps visible in the distance. Climb the steps. Just before you reach a set of gates, turn left along a narrow path to reach The Novers ★ , the first of the Northern Slopes: a broad grassy sward with spectacular views towards the Clifton Suspension Bridge. When you've had a look around, return to the steps.

**9** Go through the gates at the top of the steps to reach Knowle West Health Park. Turn left and follow the perimeter footpath, leaving the park via the gate at the northern corner. Go straight on into Clonmel Road.

**10** Cross the top of Glyn Vale and go straight on into Cavan Walk. At the far end of the cul-de-sac, take the footpath in the right corner to enter the next section of the Northern Slopes, Glyn Vale/Kenmare ★. Take the path to the left to descend through a large area of wild scrub.

**11** Leave via the gates onto Wedmore Vale. Cross Wedmore Vale, heading downhill, then turn right into Wingfield Road. On the right, look out for a narrow footpath between numbers 73 and 71 Wingfield Road. Take this path to reach The Bommie ★, the final section of the Northern Slopes.

**12** Climb the footpath until you reach a grassy clearing on the right. Strike out across the grass, following a roughly trodden footpath through the grass itself. Follow the grassy path through the lower clearings of The Bommie; soon you will dip down into a small wooded gulley, emerging at the foot of a steep grassy hill.

**13** Make your way to the top of the grassy hill. Making an anticlockwise loop around the space will allow you to take it all in. Leave The Bommie via the gates at the top, emerging on Stockwood Crescent. Turn left and make your way to busy Redcatch Road.

**14** Cross the road, turn right and then turn left to continue along Redcatch Road. Take the second left, St Agnes Avenue.

**15** Reaching a junction of five roads, turn right along Sylvia Avenue. Go straight on into Crowndale Road to return to Wells Road. Cross the road at the traffic lights, then turn left to make your way back down to Holy Nativity Church, passing shops and cafés.

# **A·Z** walk seven

## From High Street to Green Vale

The northern suburbs of St Andrews and Ashley Down.

Many of the streets and spaces of north Bristol's inner suburbs are worth exploring if you enjoy street walks. This walk is one example, combining some very pleasant residential streets with a variety of lovely green spaces, both formal and wild.

Starting at the busy Zetland Road junction, you will visit the most vibrant section of Gloucester Road, which is one of the most successful independent high streets in the country, with barely a chain store to be found.

Doubling back into the comfortable Victorian residential neighbourhood of St Andrews, you will climb up through the chilled-out St Andrew's Park to check out the great view from Ashley Down Green.

Following the Concorde Way cycle path you will then enter Ashley Vale, a green, secluded area that is home to some beautiful allotments, quirky self-build houses and the peaceful retreat of St Werburghs City Farm.

You have the option to climb up through a nature reserve at Narroways Hill, leaving paved paths for the only time on this circuit. You will then return to Gloucester Road via the unique, bohemian Georgian hillside neighbourhood of Montpelier.

| | |
|---|---|
| **start / finish** | Junction of Gloucester Road and Zetland Road, Bishopston, Bristol |
| **nearest postcode** | BS7 8AE |
| **distance** | 3 miles / 4.8 km |
| **time** | 2 hours 15 minutes |
| **terrain** | Surfaced paths and roads, with optional unsurfaced section. Moderately steep climbs and some steps. |

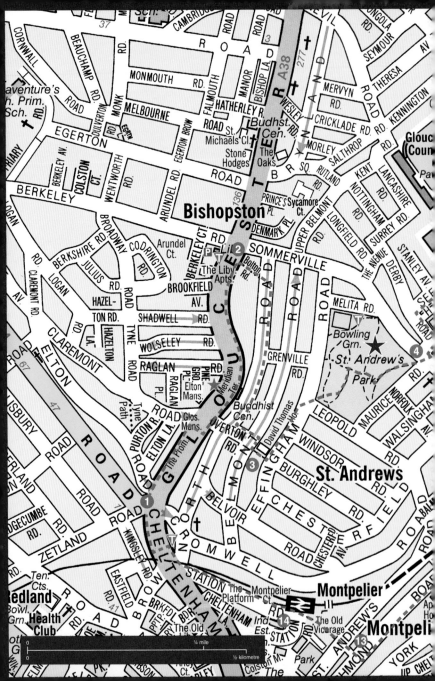

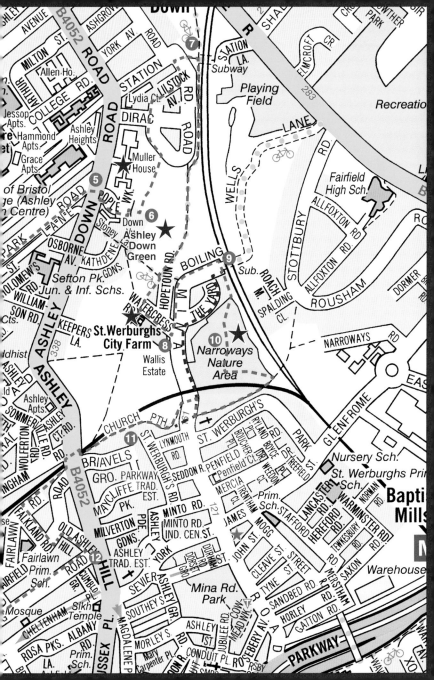

Parking in much of the area is restricted to residents only on weekdays, but there are pay and display bays on Zetland Road and at the ends of the residential streets that lead off it. Alternatively, take the short walk from Montpelier railway station (which is on the route of this walk, near the end) or Redland Station (10 minutes); or take the bus to Gloucester Road itself (bus stop 'Zetland Road junction').

**1** From the junction of Zetland Road and Gloucester Road, turn left to make your way north along Gloucester Road. Cross over at the first set of traffic lights and continue up the right-hand side of the street for the best look at the shops.

**2** Just before the second set of traffic lights, take the small lane, Bolton Road, which turns off to the right. Reaching North Road, turn right. Continue for a while then turn left up Overton Road and walk to the end.

**3** Turn right onto Belmont Road and then almost immediately left into David Thomas Lane, a small footpath. At the end, turn left again into Effingham Road and follow it until you reach St Andrew's Park ★. Make your way diagonally across the park so that you approach its highest corner, keeping the children's play area to your left.

**4** Cross Sommerville Road at the pedestrian crossing and take the nearby turning for Derby Road. Turn right onto leafy Sefton Park Road, where every house has its own name. Make your way to the far end.

**5** Reaching Ashley Down Road opposite the looming stone buildings of the former Müller Orphanage ★, carefully cross the busy road. Turn right and then left, following Pople Walk past the orphanage buildings. Turn left towards an internal courtyard, then turn right down a flight of steps in between the new-build flats and the older buildings to reach Ashley Down Green ★.

**6** Turn left and follow the path at the top of the green so that you reach Dirac Road. Continue straight on and then descend through a gap in a wall to reach Lilstock Avenue. Go down to Station Road, turn left and then make a hard right onto the Concorde Way cycle path.

**7** Follow the path, keeping the main railway line to your left. Keep going roughly straight on and you will eventually reach St Werburghs City Farm ★. Explore the farm if you like, then walk down Watercress Road.

**8** Turn left along Mina Road so that you pass a development of self-build houses. At the end of the road, bear right onto Boiling Wells Lane. Follow the lane until you approach a little tunnel under the main railway line. Stop just before the tunnel.

**9** There are two options at this point, as the paths in the Narroways Hill Nature Reserve ★ are unsurfaced and may be muddy. If you wish to keep your shoes clean, go through the first gate on the right to return to Mina Road via the self-build housing; turn left, walk through the Mina Road Tunnel and then turn right onto Church Path, where you pick up the directions at step 11. Otherwise, take the second gate on the right, following a path that climbs next to the railway line.

**10** You will emerge into a green area. Follow the path around the right-hand edge of the green. Do not turn off into the woods. Climb up onto the steep embankment ahead of you, making your way up and to the left. At the far side of the open space, you are given a choice of two railway bridges. Take the one on the right to return to Mina Road. Turn right, and then turn left along Church Path just before the Mina Road Tunnel.

**11** Church Path climbs steeply until you emerge on the main road, Ashley Hill. Cross the road at the traffic lights and take the footpath opposite, following the railway, to emerge in Fairlawn Road. Take the first left, Falkland Road, passing Fairlawn Primary School. At the end of Falkland Road, turn left into Fairfield Road and then right into Old Ashley Hill.

**12** As soon as you hit the main road, turn right again into narrow Cobourg Road. When the road starts to drop downhill, turn right onto Richmond Road. Climb the hill then take the second left, also called Richmond Road, to descend again with views towards Cotham.

**13** Shortly after The Cadbury House pub, turn right into a cobbled haulingway beneath number 45 Richmond Road to cut through to St Andrew's Road. Take the broad footpath opposite to approach Montpelier Station.

**14** Go straight on along Station Road. At the end, turn right onto Cheltenham Road, passing under a railway viaduct known as The Arches, and then cross Cheltenham Road at the traffic lights. Continue along the road to return to the Zetland Road junction.

# ⒜⒵ walk eight

## Down to the Gorge

Leafy streets and nature reserves near the Avon Gorge.

Some of the most affluent streets within the city limits can be found in Stoke Bishop and Sneyd Park, the leafy suburbs to the north of The Downs in the northwest of the city. The area is also good territory for urban walks, with quiet footpaths full of fragrant fallen leaves and pine cones.

Starting among the open spaces of The Downs, this walk follows a series of quiet lanes and paths down into the tranquil and desirable residential area of Stoke Bishop. Passing briefly through university territory, with an optional detour back up the hill to visit the University of Bristol Botanic Gardens, the route proceeds to the spacious leafy streets of Sneyd Park.

The route then ventures down into the Avon Gorge through a series of nature reserves and woodlands at Old Sneed Park, Bennett's Patch and White's Paddock, and Bishops Knoll. This section is the scenic highlight of the walk, but can be skipped if you are looking for something less strenuous. Finally, the walk climbs back up through Sneyd Park to reach the top of the Avon Gorge. The route concludes with a walk across The Downs to complete the circuit.

| | |
|---|---|
| **start / finish** | White Tree Roundabout (A4018), North View, Westbury Park, Bristol |
| **nearest postcode** | BS6 7QB |
| **distance** | 5 miles / 8 km |
| **time** | 3 hours 15 minutes |
| **terrain** | Some unsurfaced paths and grassy areas that are slippery and muddy after bad weather. Hills and steep steps. |

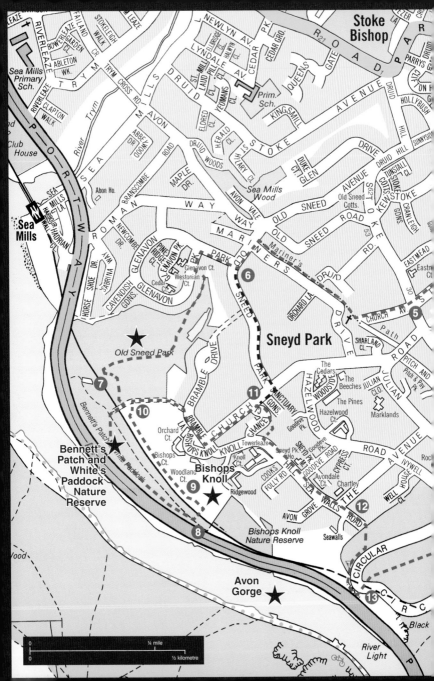

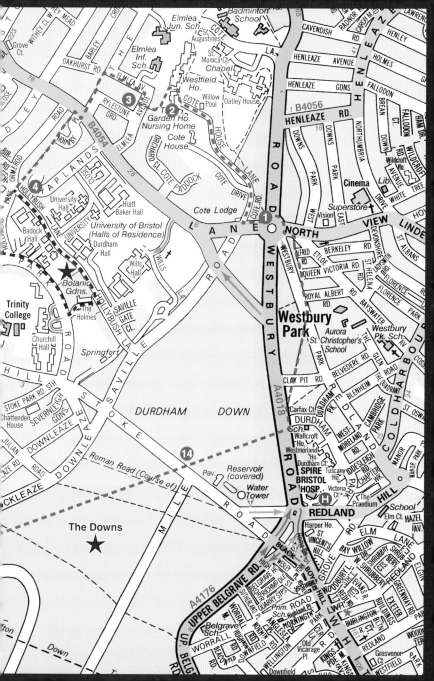

Park on Westbury Park, North View or on one of the surrounding streets; or take a bus to North View (bus stop 'Westbury Road').

**1** Start by following Parrys Lane west from the White Tree Roundabout. Turn right into Cote Road. Go straight on down Cote House Lane until the public road ends.

**2** Take the public footpath on the right that is signed to 'Elmlea Schools'. Follow the path round a corner and down a flight of steps. Turn left onto another footpath.

**3** When you reach Elmlea Avenue, turn right. At the bottom of the hill, turn left onto a footpath that is signed to 'Parrys Lane', then bear right onto Rylestone Grove. Cross Parrys Lane. Start along Hornby Place and then bear right onto another public footpath. Follow the path until you reach a junction.

**4** You have the option here to take a detour to the University of Bristol Botanic Gardens ★ : turn left and climb steep Hollybush Lane. At the top of the hill, turn right through the rear gates of a grand University property called The Holmes; the ticket kiosk is just past the house. When you've finished exploring the gardens, leave via the front gates onto Stoke Park Road, turn right and follow the road until you come out on Stoke Hill, then proceed from step 5. Otherwise, continue straight on past the Hollybush

Lane junction, following a track. Walk past the end of Little Stoke Road then bear left onto Hollymead Lane. Reaching Stoke Park Road, turn right and follow the road until you come out on Stoke Hill.

**5** Reaching the main road, Stoke Hill, cross over into Church Avenue. Outside the churchyard, turn right onto Mariners' Path. Follow the path to the far end, then turn left onto Old Sneed Park until you reach the junction with Glenavon Park.

**6** If you would prefer to skip the steep Avon Gorge section ★ , go straight on and climb Old Sneed Park. Turn right along Church Road and then left into Chancel Close to rejoin the main route at step 11. Otherwise, turn right up Glenavon Park. At the top of the slope, turn left onto another section of Glenavon Park. After a short distance, turn left down a track between stone walls leading to a gate. Make your way down through Old Sneed Park Nature Reserve ★ – don't miss the lake on the left. Continue through the nature reserve until you approach a railway embankment.

**7** Turn left through a gate and climb a footpath. Before long you will reach a gate onto a stone-walled woodland track. Turn right and make your way down the track until you reach a railway bridge. Cross the railway bridge and follow the path round to the left to enter Bennett's Patch and White's Paddock Nature Reserve ★ . Make your way through the wildflower meadow, heading back towards the railway line as the meadow narrows down.

**8** Take a narrow footpath on the left that leads to a tunnel under the railway line. Go through the gate to enter the lost gardens of Bishops Knoll ★ , a former Victorian landscaped garden whose overgrown features are being slowly rediscovered by a team of volunteers. Climb to the top of the steep steps beyond to reach the middle level of the gardens. Explore the gardens if you wish, then leave via the exit on the middle level.

**9** Go straight through an arboretum of sorts, ignoring side turnings, until you come back out on the stone-walled woodland track that you walked down earlier.

**10** Turn right and climb the track until you come out on Bramble Lane at the junction with Bramble Drive. Continue up Bramble Lane and then turn left along Church Road. Just before a row of pine trees on the left, turn right into Chancel Close.

**11** Make your way round the road to the left of the houses. At the top of the slope, where the road turns to the right, go straight on up a footpath next to a tall conifer tree. At the top of the footpath, turn left onto Knoll Hill. Climb the hill and go straight on into Sea Walls Road.

**12** Where the road turns left onto The Avenue, go straight on into a cul-de-sac section of Sea Walls Road. At the end of the road, go through the pedestrian gate to return to The Downs ★ . Bear right across the grass to reach Circular Road and follow it to the edge of the cliff to take in the view.

**13** Begin making your way back across The Downs. Set a roughly diagonal course across the grass, keeping the distant water tower just off to your right. You will converge gradually on Ladies Mile, which crosses The Downs from behind you to the right, but do not cross it. Eventually you will reach Stoke Road, the main road that crosses The Downs from left to right.

**14** Cross Stoke Road and continue on a diagonal path, making for busy Westbury Road to the right, where there is a set of traffic lights next to a bus stop. Cross Westbury Road at the traffic lights. Turn left briefly and then bear right onto a diagonal path across a smaller area of The Downs planted with trees, crossing Clay Pit Road in the process. After a while, the path converges on a street called Westbury Park. Follow Westbury Park until the junction with Royal Albert Road and then take the path that is set back from the road to the right, following the edge of the green space. Turn left onto North View to return to the White Tree Roundabout.

# **A-Z walk nine**

## **The Avon Valley**

The eastern suburbs of Crew's Hole, Conham
and St George.

The steep north side of the Avon Valley around Crew's Hole and Conham is
riddled with fascinating, little-known lanes and byways, and is also home to
the Troopers Hill Nature Reserve. The suburban expansion of St George has
encroached on many of these ancient lanes, but parts of the hillside retain a
distinctly rural feel within the city. This route explores the best of these and
also includes a pleasant walk along the bottom of the valley itself.

Starting at Avonview Cemetery on the edge of St George, you will descend
via Strawberry Lane to the spacious Avon Valley at Crew's Hole. Walking
along the river for a while, you will explore the very pretty Conham River Park
before following the Stradbrook stream as you climb back up through the
charming Conham Vale.

Returning to St George, you will explore the secluded Magpie Bottom Nature
Reserve before heading back down to the bottom of the Avon Valley via a
series of quiet streets and steps. For the final stretch, you will climb steeply
back up through the Troopers Hill Nature Reserve with its distinct ecosystem
and iconic chimney before visiting the Strawberry Lane Community Garden
on your way back to Avonview Cemetery.

| | |
|---|---|
| **start / finish** | Main entrance of Avonview Cemetery, Beaufort Road, St George, Bristol |
| **nearest postcode** | BS5 8EN |
| **distance** | 4½ miles / 7.4 km |
| **time** | 3 hours |
| **terrain** | Some unsurfaced paths, which may be slippery and muddy after bad weather. Steep hills, steps and a stile. |

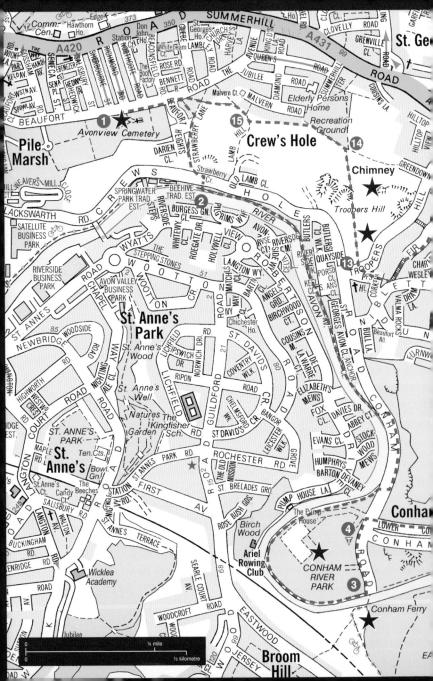

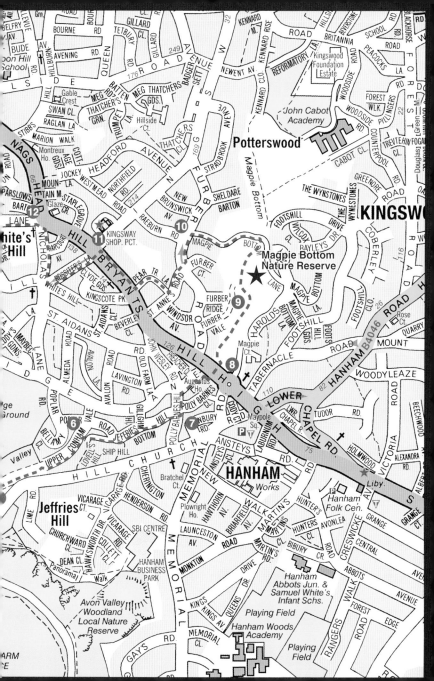

Park on Beaufort Road opposite Avonview Cemetery; or take the short walk from Lawrence Hill Railway Station (15 minutes); or take the bus to Church Road (bus stop 'Northcote Road').

**1** From the main entrance of Avonview Cemetery ★ , head east along Beaufort Road, keeping the cemetery to your right. Cross the entrance to Beaufort Heights and then immediately turn right down Strawberry Lane, a narrow footpath. At the bottom of the hill, turn left along Crews Hole Road and immediately right along a short footpath leading to the River Avon.

**2** Turn left along the path and follow the Avon upriver for a total of nearly 1¼ miles (2 km). When the riverside path merges with Conham Road, cross over. Follow the pavement until you see a footpath branching off to the right. Take this footpath to enter Conham River Park ★ . Continue to follow the riverside footpath around a long bend in the river.

**3** Shortly after passing a stone railway viaduct on the far bank, you will reach Conham Ferry ★ , where a tiny ferry boat runs passengers across the river during the summer months to reach the popular tearoom on the far side. Take the broad track that leads away from the river next to the ferry. The track takes you back to Conham Road.

**4** Climb over the stile at the end of the track to access the road. Go straight on for a moment then turn right into Lower Conham Vale, passing a few cottages. Follow the charming valley route as it continues beyond the houses, climbing next to the Stradbrook stream.

**5** Don't get sidetracked by the steps that branch off to the right, up towards Conham Hill: instead, continue along the lower route. After passing a large, hidden garden, you will come out on Upper Conham Vale. Turn right and climb the quiet road.

**6** After you have passed the last of the cottages on the right, turn right down a narrow flight of steps. Continue straight on along Jeffries Hill Bottom, which varies in width and character as you go along. Ignore any footpaths or roads that climb up out of the valley.

**7** When you get to the crossroads where Jeffries Hill Bottom meets Polly Barnes Hill, turn left. Climb the hill and then turn right into Dundridge Lane. Follow Dundridge Lane until it ends at a car park just below the main road, Bryants Hill. Climb a few steps to reach the main road and cross over.

**8** Go through the gates opposite to enter Magpie Bottom Nature Reserve ★ . Follow the gravel path round to the left. When the main path turns to cross the stream, take the smaller path ahead of you instead.

**9** Stay on the left-hand side of the stream. Keep going straight on, following the waterway, passing two white-painted footbridges. Eventually you will emerge at a T junction of sorts next to a third white-painted structure crossing the stream. Take the left turn, signed to the 'Magpie Bottom Nature Reserve Orchard', so that you climb out of the valley via Magpie Bottom Lane. Continue climbing, sticking to the main path, until you emerge on a paved stretch of road with a few bungalows. Follow this lane to emerge on Furber Road.

**10** Turn left onto Furber Road and take the second right, St Anne's Road. About halfway down St Anne's Road, at the crest of the hill, turn right through a gap between house numbers 25 and 23 to reach Pear Tree Lane. Follow the lane round until you return to Bryants Hill. Turn right.

**11** When you reach a crossroads with traffic lights, carefully cross the main road and turn left into Rossiter's Lane and walk to the end. Turn right into Nicholas Lane to return to the main road once again and then immediately turn left into Fir Tree Lane.

**12** Follow Fir Tree Lane until it turns into a flight of steps. Descend the steps to reach Niblett's Hill. Immediately turn right onto another flight of steps, Parfitt's Hill, which will eventually bring you out at the bottom of the valley, close to the junction of Crews Hole Road and Trooper's Hill Road.

**13** Cross the bottom of Trooper's Hill Road and take the footpath opposite. Climb the steep steps up onto Troopers Hill Nature Reserve ★ . Stick to the main path, climbing the steps to the left of the main open area. If you wish, take a detour to look inside the chimney ★ , which is a remnant of the 18th-century copper smelting industry. Exit the nature reserve via the gate to the left of the chimney, at the top of the hill.

**14** Follow the path along the lower edge of Troopers Hill Field and go through the pedestrian gate to the left of the houses on Malvern Road. Walk through the woods and then turn right up the next footpath, Lamb Hill.

**15** Reaching a tarmac driveway, go straight across and onto another stretch of footpath, going down a few steps. Take the left fork so that you pass through Strawberry Lane Community Garden. Continue straight on, ignoring side turnings, and you will eventually emerge on Beaufort Road at the top of Strawberry Lane. Go straight on along Beaufort Road to return to Avonview Cemetery.

# ᴀᴢ walk ten

## The Peaceful Valley

The northern suburbs of Henleaze and
Westbury-on-Trym.

Over the centuries, the city of Bristol has expanded to absorb several
surrounding villages. Today, the best-preserved of these old village centres is
probably Westbury-on-Trym. Nestled in the wooded valley of the River Trym,
the village retains much of the peaceful charm of a rural settlement.

Starting in the traditional Edwardian high street of Henleaze, this route
makes its way towards Westbury-on-Trym via a series of desirable leafy
streets. Reaching the Trym Valley, the route takes a detour upstream to
explore the Badocks Wood Nature Reserve with its pleasant mix of ancient
woodland and meadows. It then follows a secluded lane to reach the centre
of Westbury-on-Trym itself.

The route explores the old village centre in depth, climbing in and out of the
valley several times to reveal its many fascinating lanes and steps and the
peaceful surroundings of Holy Trinity Church.

After a brief visit to Westbury-on-Trym's high street, the walk climbs back
out of the valley one last time, taking a detour past two historic private
schools and the grand buildings of the St Monica retirement community on
the way back to Henleaze.

| | |
|---|---|
| **start / finish** | Junction of Henleaze Road and Henleaze Avenue, Henleaze, Bristol |
| **nearest postcode** | BS9 4JY |
| **distance** | 4¼ miles / 6.8 km |
| **time** | 2 hours 30 minutes |
| **terrain** | Mostly paved or gravel paths and roads, with some grassy areas. Hills, one stile and some steep steps. |

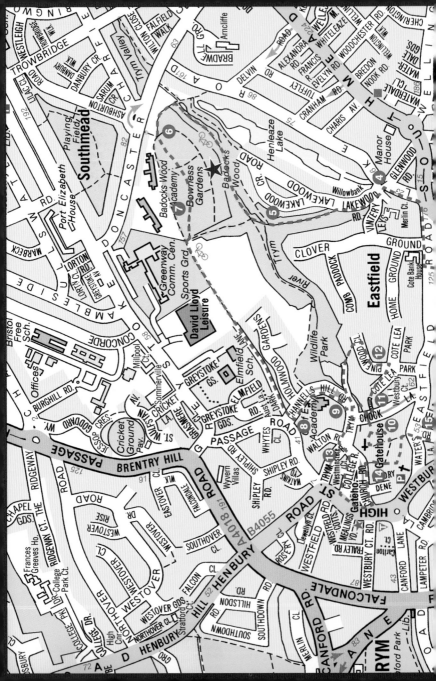

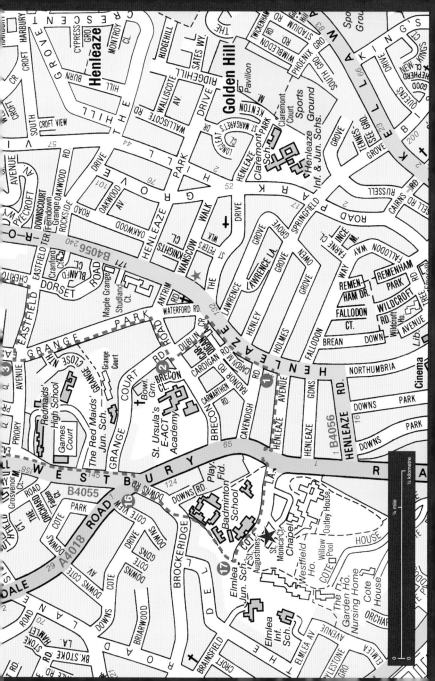

Park on one of the side streets off the top end of Henleaze Road; or take a bus to Henleaze Road (bus stop 'Henley Grove').

**1** From the corner of Henleaze Avenue, start by heading down through the shops on Henleaze Road. Just before the petrol station, make a hard left into Dublin Crescent and walk to the end.

**2** Turn right along Brecon Road to reach a crossroads. Note the thatched lodge in the distance, then turn left into Grange Park and walk to the end.

**3** Turn right into Eastfield. Take the first left into Cheriton Place. Walk to the end then turn right onto the main road, Eastfield Road. Follow Eastfield Road down the hill until you reach a roundabout, then turn left into Lake Road.

**4** Take the left turn into Lakewood Road. Head north on Lakewood Road with woodland to your left and a modern block of flats to your right. After a few metres, turn left through a gate to enter Badocks Wood ★ , descending next to a stream. Follow the footpath to the bottom of the hill.

**5** At a crossing of paths, turn right along a tarmac path with the River Trym to your right. At the far end, turn left up another path, climbing gently until you reach another crossing of paths in a more open area at the top of the hill.

**6** Take the rough path that goes straight on from the crossroads. Go straight on along a grassy path through the first meadow, heading for a gap in the hedge. Cross the second meadow in a similar fashion. You will reach a triangle where several paths meet next a Bronze Age round barrow.

**7** Follow the path around the barrow. You will emerge at the top of a tarmac path which leads back down into the valley. Cross this path and enter the open field beyond. Walk across the field, staying close to the hedge line on the right. At the far end of the field, go in among the trees on the right to find a gate leading to Dark Lane. Follow the lane until you emerge on Passage Road.

**8** Immediately turn left into Channells Hill and make your way down into Westbury Village. Turn right along Trym Road next to the river.

**9** Cross the second of two small stone bridges on the left so that you walk through a little garden area. Cross Chock Lane and climb the footpath opposite to approach the church.

**10** At the top of the footpath, just outside the churchyard gates, turn left onto another footpath. Climb briefly to enter the churchyard via the top gate. Explore the churchyard as you head back down, then turn right and retrace your steps to Chock Lane.

**11** Turn right and climb the raised pavement on the left-hand side of Chock Lane, opposite The Victoria Inn. Turn left and climb a steep flight of steps, reaching Cote Lea Park. Follow the road. At a crossroads, turn left into Pinewood Close.

**12** Follow Pinewood Close round the bend until you reach a footpath leading back down into the valley. Turn left down the footpath. You will eventually return to Trym Road. This time, go straight on past the junction with Chock Lane.

**13** Reaching another junction, turn left across the river into Church Road and then bear right into College Road, passing the remains of the 15th-century Westbury College. Turn left into High Street for a quick look at the village centre, then turn left again into Church Road.

**14** When Church Road slews off back towards the river, go straight on towards the church. Turn right onto the footpath just outside the church gates. When the footpath makes a sharp left, go straight on into a garden area. Climb the gravel footpath through the centre of the gardens and then turn right onto a tarmac path to reach the main road at the top of Waters Lane.

**15** Very carefully cross the top of Waters Lane to reach a quieter section of Eastfield Road. Follow Eastfield Road until it merges with Westbury Hill. Go straight on along Westbury Road, passing Redmaids' High School.

**16** At the busy junction where Westbury Road merges with fast-flowing Falcondale Road, cross the top of Falcondale Road and take the right fork into quieter Downs Road. You will reach a second fork where Downs Road continues as a cul-de-sac on the left and Great Brockeridge descends to the right. Take the footpath at the centre of the fork.

**17** The path will eventually lead you to a stile at the bottom of Cote Lane. Cross the stile and turn left up Cote Lane itself, passing between Badminton School and the imposing buildings of St Monica's ★ . Cross busy Westbury Road at the zebra crossing and go straight on along Henleaze Avenue to return to Henleaze Road.

# ᴬᶻ walk eleven

## Frome Valley and its Villages

The River Frome from Stapleton to Frenchay.

This highly scenic walk explores the steep-sided valley of the Frome, one of Bristol's main rivers.

Starting on the approach to the village of Stapleton, 2½ miles (4 km) northeast of Bristol city centre, the route begins with a view of the elegant Holy Trinity Church and a detour through a pleasant wildflower meadow with views of the Purdown ridge.

The route then joins the course of the River Frome and follows the popular riverside walkway through Eastville Park, passing its Edwardian boating lake.

After a walk up Wickham Hill, the route rejoins the river at Snuff Mills, in the heart of the wooded Frome Valley. Proceeding to Oldbury Court Estate, passing weirs and rapids, the route takes you all the way to the picturesque village of Frenchay, which retains a lot of its old, rural charm.

After a circuit around Frenchay, the return journey wanders in and out of the valley, taking in some of the quieter lanes that run up and down the sides of the valley. You will glimpse the buildings of St Matthias' College, several tucked-away old cottages and a little more of the village of Stapleton.

| | |
|---|---|
| **start / finish** | Lay-by on Bell Hill, Stapleton |
| **nearest postcode** | BS16 1BE |
| **distance** | 6¾ miles / 10.9 km |
| **time** | 4 hours |
| **terrain** | Some unsurfaced paths that may be slippery and muddy after bad weather. Steep hills and some steps. |

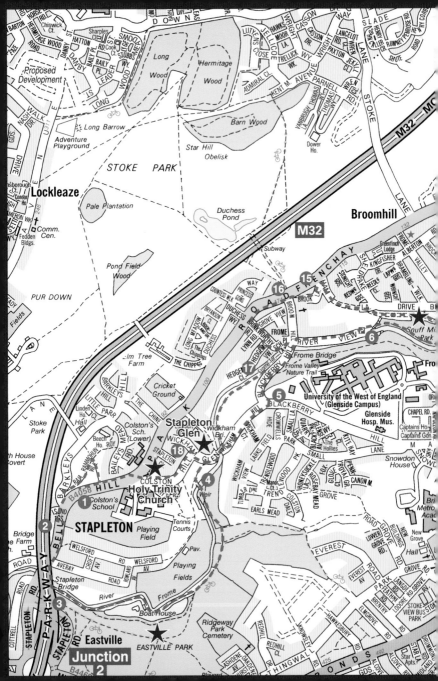

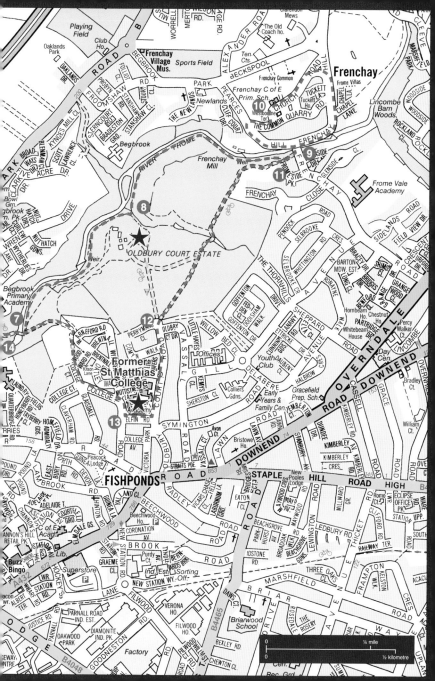

Park in the lay-by halfway along Bell Hill; or take the bus to Bell Hill (bus stop 'Stapleton Church').

**1** From the lay-by, climb towards the church. After passing the first couple of houses, take the narrow footpath that leads off to the left near the bus stop. At a crossroads of footpaths, go left and descend through a wildflower meadow to return to Bell Hill.

**2** Cross Bell Hill and walk down the road until you reach a bridge over the River Frome underneath the M32 viaduct. Cross the bridge and turn left along the shared pedestrian/cycle path that runs alongside the river.

**3** Follow the path to the former boating lake in Eastville Park ★. Stick to the left-hand side of the lake, passing the remains of the boathouse. Continue along the riverside until you reach a narrow footbridge over the river.

**4** Cross the footbridge and follow the river path to the right, emerging on the narrow lane of Wickham Glen. Turn right and cross historic Wickham Bridge at the heart of the quiet Stapleton Glen ★. Continue straight on into Wickham Hill, climbing past old buildings and gas lamps to reach the road named Blackberry Hill.

**5** Cross Blackberry Hill and make your way back down to the bottom of the valley, reaching Frome Bridge. Cross the bridge and turn right into River View to reach the Snuff Mills car park.

**6** Take the riverside walkway once again. Make your way through the Snuff Mills ★. Despite the name, tobacco snuff was never ground here; the mill was used for crushing locally quarried stone. You will pass a cottage, gardens and an old mill before reaching an old footbridge known as the Halfpenny Bridge.

**7** Cross the Halfpenny Bridge and turn left to continue following the river, which is now to your left, entering Oldbury Court Estate ★, which was sold to Bristol Corporation by the last descendant of the Vassall family in 1937, for use as a public park. Shortly after passing a weir, you will reach a major junction in the footpath where a smaller stream joins the Frome from the right.

**8** Stay on the riverside path, looking out for slippery rocks and muddy patches. At length, a flight of steps will bring you out at Frenchay Bridge.

**9** Cross the bridge and then turn right along Frenchay Hill to complete a circuit of picturesque Frenchay Village. At the top of the hill, take the path on the left next to the former telephone box to reach Church Road. Continue straight on until you come out on the edge of Frenchay Common.

**10** Turn left into Westbourne Terrace and then right past the White Lion pub. At the end of the road, turn left onto Pearces Hill and make your way back down to Frenchay Bridge.

**11** Cross back over the bridge and take the footpath leading off to the right: not the riverside walkway, but the wider track that climbs up to the top of Oldbury Court Estate. After you have crossed a tree-lined stream, take the left fork to reach the Oldbury Court Estate car park.

**12** Turn left into Oldbury Court Road. Follow the road until you reach the buildings of the former St Matthias' College ★, originally the Gloucester and Bristol Diocesan Training Institution for School Mistresses. Turn right into Elfin Road.

**13** Turn right into College Road and follow it along the back of the college. Bear left and continue along College Road. Opposite the junction with Glaisdale Road, turn right onto a footpath signed for the Frome Valley, which runs between a small paddock and a high stone wall concealing a row of modern garages. Follow the path back down to the Halfpenny Bridge.

**14** Cross the bridge once again and go straight on along a track, climbing the far side of the valley. At the far end, turn left onto Ham Lane, which quickly becomes a rugged woodland track before passing a row of cottages.

**15** As Ham Lane joins the main road, make a hard left, so that you double back into Brook Lane. Descend the footpath at the far end of Brook Lane to reach a mini-roundabout at the lower gates to Stoke Park Estate.

**16** Cross the top of Broom Hill and follow busy Park Road. After a short distance, turn left into Brinkworthy Road. At the end of the road, turn right into Hedgemead View and immediately left onto a paved lane that descends further into the valley, returning to Frome Bridge. Cross the bridge once again and make your way up Blackberry Hill, climbing past Frome Terrace until you see a cycle path on the right.

**17** Take the cycle path, leaving the road behind you, to return along the riverside to Stapleton Glen at Wickham Bridge. Cross the bridge and follow Wickham Glen round to the right.

**18** Reaching a wooded junction, turn left onto Colston Hill. Climb the quiet lane to return to Stapleton Village, reaching a tiny village green area to the rear of Holy Trinity Church ★. Continue straight on to reach Bell Hill and make your way back down to the lay-by.

# **Az** walk twelve

## The Folly Castle

Blaise Castle Estate and Coombe Dingle.

The sprawling Blaise Castle Estate is a great asset to north Bristol, providing a large and diverse country park within the city limits. As well as recreational grassy areas, the estate has extensive woodlands, a lovely river valley and one of the best children's playgrounds in the city. There are also several built features of interest.

This route starts with a detour outside the estate to visit the fairytale oddity of Blaise Hamlet and the historic buildings of Henbury village, including the parish church.

Returning to the estate, the walk passes Blaise Castle House (now a museum) and climbs up through woodlands to reach the quirky folly of Blaise Castle itself. Taking in the view over Henbury Gorge from Lovers Leap, the route then descends into the gorge itself, passing Stratford Mill.

The route follows the length of the valley to Coombe Dingle, following Hazel Brook. The route then takes to leafy, desirable residential roads for a while as it climbs back up towards Kings Weston Hill. After passing the earthworks of an ancient hillfort, the route descends back into the main part of Blaise Castle Estate to return to the car park.

| | |
|---|---|
| **start / finish** | Blaise Castle car park, Kings Weston Road, Henbury, Bristol |
| **nearest postcode** | BS10 7QT |
| **distance** | 3¾ miles / 6.1 km |
| **time** | 2 hours 30 minutes |
| **terrain** | Some unsurfaced paths and grassy areas that are slippery and muddy after bad weather. Hills and steps. |

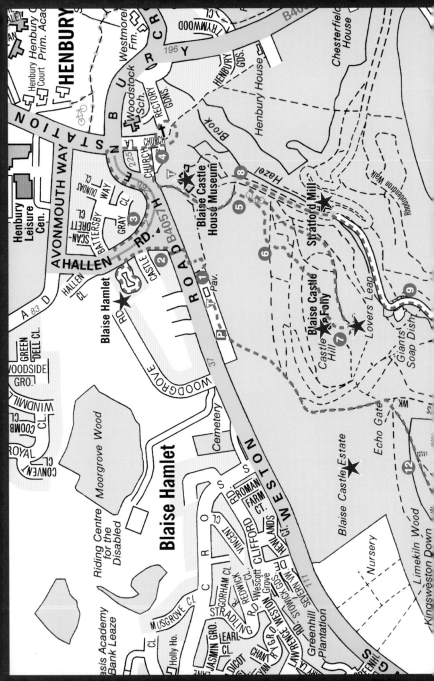

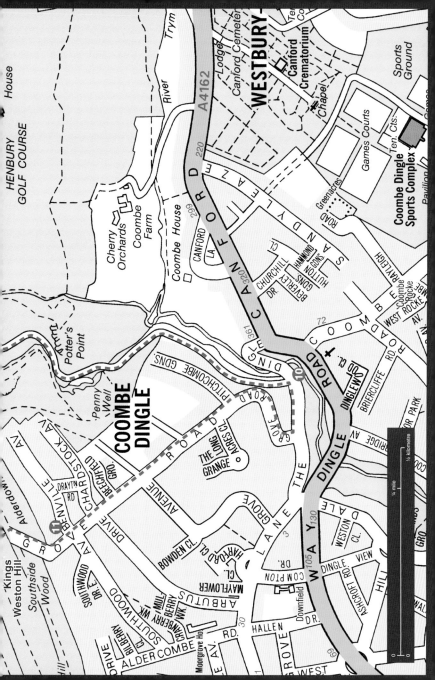

Park in the main Blaise Castle car park, which extends onto the grass in the summer; or take a bus to Kings Weston Road (bus stop 'Blaise Castle').

**1** Take the footpath from the southeast corner of the car park, close to the buildings. Turn left onto a path running between the café and the play area to reach Kings Weston Road. Turn right along Kings Weston Road. When a pavement appears on the other side, carefully cross the road and continue to the next junction.

**2** Turn left into Hallen Road. Cross the end of Castle Close and then go through the gate a little further down the hill to reach Blaise Hamlet ★ . Take a walk around the hamlet to see the picturesque cottages built to house the retired staff of Blaise Castle Estate, then cross Hallen Road and walk back up to the junction.

**3** Bear left onto Henbury Road to walk down the old main street of Henbury village. At the bottom of the hill, just before you reach a mini-roundabout, turn right into Church Lane. Climb up the lane to reach St Mary's Church. Take a walk around the churchyard and return to Church Lane.

**4** Turn left into the upper section of Church Lane to return to Henbury Road. Turn immediately left through the large gates to enter Blaise Castle Estate ★ via the stables entrance. Follow the driveway until you reach the open grassy area of the estate. Passing the museum ★ , bear left so that you follow the main drive gently down towards the woods.

**5** At the very edge of the woods, turn right onto the path that runs along the woodland edge of the grassy area. After a short while, the path enters the treeline. You will pass a small marker showing a crude picture of a castle. The path then bears right and immediately left. You will quickly reach a point where two paths turn left into the woods next to each other. Take the first, a dirt path signed with another small marker.

**6** Almost immediately you will come upon a third small marker on the right-hand side of the path. Look to the right at this marker and, a short distance up the hill, you should see the beginnings of a rough stairway leading up through the trees. Turn right and make for this staircase. Crossing the end of a carriage drive through the woods, continue past the tree stump and go straight up the path beyond, passing redwood trees, to reach Blaise Castle ★ itself.

**7** Turn left outside the castle doors and descend the short dirt slope opposite to reach a viewpoint known as Lovers Leap ★ . Turn left at the fence and take the path that traverses the steep hillside. After a short while you will pass a small cave lined with a stone seat. Continue straight on, ignoring all the informal and occasionally treacherous side paths and shortcuts. At length you will descend a short flight of steps to rejoin the main drive on the way down into the valley.

**8** Turn right, descending into Henbury Gorge. You will pass the historic Stratford Mill ★ , moved to this location in 1956 when its original site was submerged during the creation of Chew Valley Lake in Somerset. After crossing a bridge, turn right to follow the pedestrian and cycle path on down the valley, keeping the Hazel Brook to your right. After a while, the valley opens out around the first of a series of pretty ponds. Do not cross the water here; instead, continue along the main path, keeping the water to your right.

**9** The path climbs again towards an area known as the Beech Cathedral before descending again past another pond. Continue to stay on the main path, avoiding side turnings. After a while, the main path will take you across the Hazel Brook. Continue following the path until you eventually emerge in the Coombe Dingle car park.

**10** Turn right onto The Dingle. Climb the hill and take the first right, Grove Road, which heads in among the houses. The road twists and turns at first before straightening out into a gentle climb. The character of the road changes repeatedly between suburban street and country lane. Climb all the way to the junction with Southwood Avenue, just below the treeline.

**11** Continue climbing as Grove Road turns into a track. Follow this track up through an area of woodland. Avoid any side turnings in the woods and you will soon come out on a grassy area at the top of Kings Weston Hill ★ . Turn right along the ridge to reach the remaining earthworks of an Iron Age hillfort.

**12** Go through a small opening into the woods on the left, next to the remains of an iron fence or gate. The path will take you to a broad stairway leading down through a fairly open area of woodland. Keep going straight on until you reach a path leading out into the open. Turn left into a grassy area, passing the dead remains of two large trees. Follow the grassy area on round the corner, keeping the woods to your right, to reach the main grassy area of Blaise Castle Estate and return to the car park.

# ᴀᴢ walk thirteen

# The Heart of Bath

Quiet corners among the busy streets.

The historic heart of Bath contrasts graceful Georgian streets with a maze of hidden alleyways and arcades. Some of these are busy with tourists and shoppers; others are quieter and more tucked-away. What unifies them all is the characteristic honey-coloured Bath Stone, which has been used as a building material throughout all eras from Roman to modern.

This walk tours the heart of the city via a mix of busy spaces and quieter routes. Starting at Bath Spa Station, you will enter the city centre via the redeveloped SouthGate shopping centre before paying a visit to the lively surrounds of Bath Abbey and the ancient Roman Baths. Walking via a couple of narrow passageways you will pay a visit to the hidden Bath Markets (open Monday to Saturday) and the historic Pulteney Bridge.

After a stroll up gracious Milsom Street with its historic Jolly's department store, you will pay a visit to Queen Square and the newly pedestrianized surroundings of the Theatre Royal. From there you will explore some of the quiet, less-visited lanes around the Thermae Bath Spa before returning to Bath Spa Station via the SouthGate centre once again.

| | |
|---|---|
| **start / finish** | Brunel Square, Dorchester Street, Bath |
| **nearest postcode** | BA1 1SX |
| **distance** | 1½ miles / 2.6 km |
| **time** | 1 hour |
| **terrain** | All surfaced roads and paths. |

PARK

HENRIETTA

CONNAUGHT MANSIONS

HENRIETTA STREET

HENRIETTA PL.
OLD GAOL

ST. JO

GROVE

CAXTON CT.

AURA
ARGYLE PLACE
JOHNSTONE ST.
GREAT

Beazer Gdn.
Maze

Bath R
Recreation
(Stand

Bath S
Leisur

Parade

SPRING GDS. RD.
Weir
Boat Trips
RIVER

Pulteney Bridge
PULTENEY
BRI.

GRAND PDE

5

Lib.

THE PODIUM

Gall.
Guildhall Mkt.
Guildhall

BRIDGE STREET

HGIH
ST.

ROAD

WALCOT STREET

NORTHGATE ST.

THE TRAMSHED

BEEHIVE

LOOP

P

WALCOT

SARACEN ST.

BROAD ST. PL.

BROAD ST.

BLADUD
YMCA

NEW BOND ST. PL.
BURTON S.

NEW BOND ST.

BOROUGH WALLS

NORTH-UMBERLAND PLACE

THE CORRIDOR

UNION ST.
UNION PASSAGE

6

CHEAP ST.

YORK BLDGS.

P

MILES PL.
M
IRES YD.

GREEN MUS.

OLD BOND S.

PARSONAGE

H

BRIDEWELL LA.
P
media
Bath

MILSOM

The Studio.

QUIET S.

QUEEN ST.
TRIM PL.
TRIM ST.
BRI.
UP.
SAWCLOSE

SEVEN

ST. ANDREWS TER.
BARTLETT ST.
EDGAR BLDGS.
MILES'S BLDGS.
BARTLETT ST.
DOWN M.

GEORGE ST.

7

BARTON BLDGS.

Jane Austen Cen.

OLD KING ST.

JOHN ST.

WOOD ST.
JOHN S.

BARTON ST.

SAWCLOSE
Theatres

ST. JOHNS PL.

GAY STREET

Georgian Garden

GAY ST.

WALK

Acad
QUEENS PDE. PL.

QUEEN SQ.

AVENUE
QUEENS PDE.
QUEEN PDE. PL.

PRINCES ST.

BEAUFORD SQ.

CHAPEL ROW

MONMOUTH ST.

ROSEWELL CT.

Offi

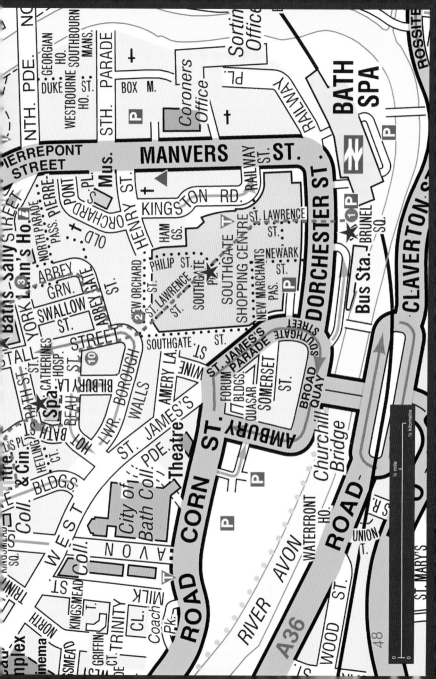

The walk starts outside Bath Spa railway station. Parking is available at nearby Avon Street Car Park and other city centre car parks. Alternatively, you can take any bus to Dorchester Street or Bath Bus Station.

**1** Starting in Brunel Square ★ outside the railway station, surrounded by bars and restaurants, begin by crossing Dorchester Street at the traffic lights. Enter the redeveloped SouthGate shopping centre ★ via St Lawrence Street. At the heart of the shopping centre, bear left and continue following St Lawrence Street until it emerges at a junction of five streets.

**2** Bear right up Stall Street and then take the first right into Abbey Gate Street. Proceed to the end of the street and turn left through an archway to enter the Abbey Green with its enormous London plane tree. Leave via Abbey Street, at the left-hand side of the square, for the best view of Bath Abbey ★ itself as you reach York Street.

**3** Cross York Street and proceed towards the front of the abbey, passing the famous Roman Baths ★ on the left. Turn left in front of the abbey, passing the entrance to the Roman Baths. Opposite the Pump Room, turn right into an alley and walk through an arch to reach Cheap Street.

**4** Cross the road and go straight on into narrow Union Passage. Turn right into a shopping arcade aptly named The Corridor. Coming out on High Street opposite the Guildhall, cross over at the traffic lights. Turn left briefly and then step through the first door on the right to enter the Bath Markets ★ . Make your way through the markets to the opposite side, where you come out on the Grand Parade, then turn left for a view of the historic Pulteney Bridge ★ .

**5** Turn left along Bridge Street. Crossing High Street again, turn left. Just before you get back to The Corridor, turn down a narrow little tunnel on the right to reach Northumberland Place. Continue straight on across Union Passage to reach Union Street.

**6** Turn right into Union Street, then cross Upper Borough Walls to reach New Bond Street via the short Burton Street. Turn left to walk round into Milsom Street, which is Bath's grandest and best-known shopping street. Optionally, as you go, check out the quirky alleyways of Milsom Place ★ on the right.

**7** At the end of Milsom Street, turn left into George Street and left again into Gay Street to reach Queen Square. Continue down the left-hand side of Queen Square and straight on into Barton Street to reach Sawclose, a public square outside the Theatre Royal ★.

**8** Descend Sawclose. Go straight on into Westgate Street and turn left through a little pocket park, following Westgate Buildings and passing the Little Theatre on the left.

**9** Turn right into Hot Bath Street, following the meandering cobbled roadway round past the Thermae Bath Spa complex ★. Just after the spa, turn left into Beau Street and continue to the end.

**10** Turn right into Stall Street. Returning to the SouthGate shopping centre, bear left into St Lawrence Street and retrace your steps to Bath Spa Station.

# **AZ** walk fourteen

## Bath's Waterways

The River Avon and the Kennet & Avon Canal.

Follow the old waterways through any city centre and you're likely to see the city's more industrial face at some point, and Bath is no exception. The city is the terminus of the Kennet & Avon Canal, which connects it with Reading. At Bath, a series of lock gates disgorge the canal traffic into the River Avon, which takes over as the main navigable waterway for the onward journey to Bristol. Downstream of the canal entrance, several industries developed along the riverside, taking advantage of its strategic importance.

The historic city centre turns its back on the river to some extent, but this riverside walk provides an interesting alternative perspective on Bath. Not all of it is picturesque, but it is certainly different.

Starting outside Bath Spa Station you will begin by following the river upstream of the canal entrance, which is the more picturesque section, providing unique views of the Parade Gardens and Pulteney Weir and Bridge. You will then cross the city centre to rejoin the river further downstream, returning through more industrial surroundings until you reach the quiet leafiness of Green Park and the regenerated Riverside Parade.

| | |
|---|---|
| **start / finish** | Brunel Square, Dorchester Street, Bath |
| **nearest postcode** | BA1 1SX |
| **distance** | 2¼ miles / 3.7 km |
| **time** | 1 hour 15 minutes |
| **terrain** | All surfaced roads and paths, some steps. |

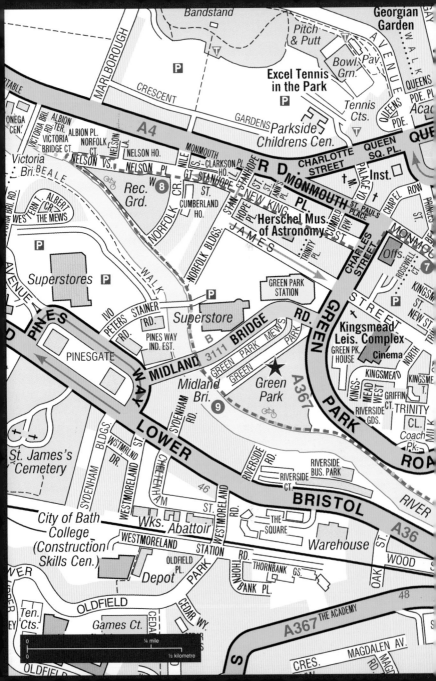

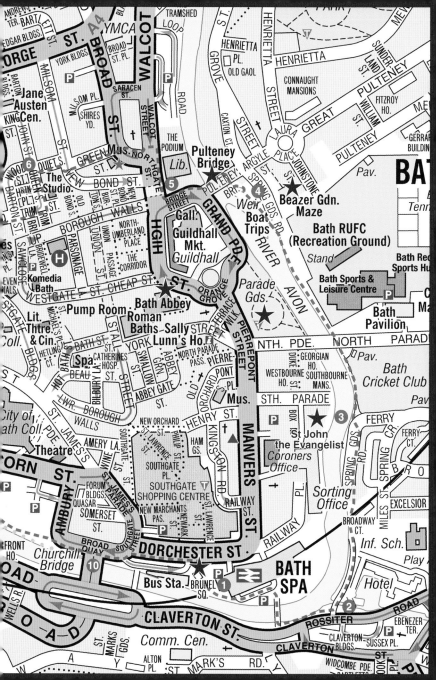

The walk starts outside Bath Spa railway station. Parking is available at nearby Avon Street Car Park and other city centre car parks. Alternatively, you can take any bus to Dorchester Street or Bath Bus Station.

**1** Starting in Brunel Square ★ outside the railway station, surrounded by bars and restaurants, begin by taking the pedestrian tunnel under the railway lines. Cross the little car park at the back of the station and then turn right across the Halfpenny Bridge. Turn left along the river, following Rossiter Road.

**2** Take the first left, crossing a little road bridge over the entrance to the Kennet & Avon Canal. Continue along the river, passing under a railway viaduct with unusual brickwork, to reach Spring Gardens Road. The church on the left is St John the Evangelist ★ .

**3** At the far end of Spring Gardens Road, continue along the river, passing first Bath Cricket Club and then Bath Rugby Club. Passing under the North Parade Bridge you will have an attractive view of Bath Abbey ★ and the Parade Gardens ★ to the left, while the historic Pulteney Weir and Bridge loom in the distance.

**4** Eventually, you will reach a quiet area of gravel and trees next to Pulteney Bridge ★ . On the right you will find the quirky Beazer Garden Maze ★ . Climb the narrow flight of steps next to Pulteney Bridge, passing under buildings to come out on the bridge itself. Turn left and cross the bridge; continue to the end of Bridge Street.

**5** Turn right into Northgate Street then left in front of St Michael's Church, crossing two roads to reach Green Street. Reaching Milsom Street in the heart of the shopping district, turn right and immediately left into Quiet Street.

**6** At the end of Quiet Street, turn left and follow Queen Street until you have passed under an archway, then turn right into Trim Street. Go straight on into historic Beauford Square, then bear left at Princes Street to reach Monmouth Street.

**7** Turn right into Monmouth Street and then left into busy Charles Street until you reach the traffic lights at the bottom of the hill. Cross the road and take New King Street opposite. Continue straight on into Great Stanhope Street, eventually reaching the unexpectedly grand Norfolk Crescent complete with historic guard post.

**8** Go straight on into Nelson Place West and you will eventually come out on a path alongside the River Avon. On the far side of the river, the modern lines of the new Western Riverside development loom beside the water. Turn left to start heading back towards the city centre, passing through a more industrial part of town.

**9** After a while you will reach the corner of Green Park ★ , a pleasant tree-lined space on the edge of the city centre. Continue along the path at the water's edge and you will eventually reach the regenerated Riverside Parade. On the far side of the river, you can see the last few historic waterfront warehouses, some of which still have housings projecting over the water from which goods would once have been hoisted to or from cargo boats. Make your way up through the shrubs to reach Broad Quay.

**10** Carefully cross the road at the end of Churchill Bridge. From there simply walk around the outside of the bus station, bearing right along Dorchester Street to return to Brunel Square.

# **AZ walk fifteen**

## **Crescents, Circles and Squares**

Georgian terraces and green spaces north of Bath
city centre.

Behind the popular visitor sights of the Royal Crescent, Royal Victoria Park
and The Circus lie a succession of quieter gardens and streets as you climb
the hill below the suburb of Lansdown.

Starting at Queen Square in the centre of Bath, this walk takes you to the
famous Royal Crescent before you head into the spacious surrounds of
Royal Victoria Park. Climbing again, you will take in the colourful Botanical
Gardens and the coniferous seclusion of the Great Dell.

Following the Cotswold Way up through the Bath Approach Golf Course
(also called the High Common), enjoying city views, you will reach the quiet
residential neighbourhood of Sion Hill.

Proceeding along the ridge to the graceful crescent of Somerset Place, you
will descend zig-zag style through a tucked-away footpath and a succession
of steep Georgian streets and quiet garden squares, eventually ending up in
the dignified surrounds of The Circus before returning to Queen Square.

| | |
|---|---|
| **start / finish** | Queen Square, Bath |
| **nearest postcode** | BA1 2HX |
| **distance** | 3 miles / 5 km |
| **time** | 2 hours |
| **terrain** | All surfaced roads and paths apart from one optional section. Some steps and one significant uphill climb. |

**Bath Spa Univ. Coll.**

SION HILL RD.

The Royal High Junior School

CRANWELLS PK.

PARK

**Sion Hill**

⑥

LINDEN GDNS.

Elmbrook

**CRANWELLS PK.**

Meriden

Victoria

CRANHILL ROAD

**HIGH COMMON**

WEST HO. ON PARK

**BATH APPROACH GOLF COURSE**

ROA

Club Ho.

⑤

OAKFIELD

PARK GARDENS

★

*Great Dell*

④

**PARK**

AUDLEY CT.

Audley Lodge

ROAD

WESTHALL RD.

LANE

**Botanical Gardens** ★

CHILDRENS

*ROYAL VICTORIA PARK AV.*

③

★

DLEY AVE.

ST. MICHAEL'S RD.

**CORK TER.**

TENNYSON RD.

CORK ST.

CORONATN.

VICTORIA PL.

RD.

COW LANE

⊽ *Playground*

**BRISTOL**

*Lower Common*

MARLBOROUGH LA.

RAIN'S RD.

Windsor

Augusta Pl.

Kelso Pl.

**VICTORIA PK. BUS. CEN.**

RIVER

AVON

MIDLAND RD.

Albion Buildings

Sovereign Point

AR Cen.

Comfortable

PL.

Albion A4 Ter.

Albion Pl.

NELSON

Windsor Ct.

STABLE YD.

OR BRI. RD.

B3604

**Phase One**

Onega Ter.

Royal Vw.

VICTORIA BRI. RD.

BRI. R.

NELSON N.

VS.

Nels

Sto rk

he Grain

ELIZABETH PDE.

Leopold

ONGMEAD T.

Highgate

Palladian

Imperial

BEALE

ALBERT

W. STN.

THE C

Rec. G.

0 ¼ mile

0 ¼ kilometre

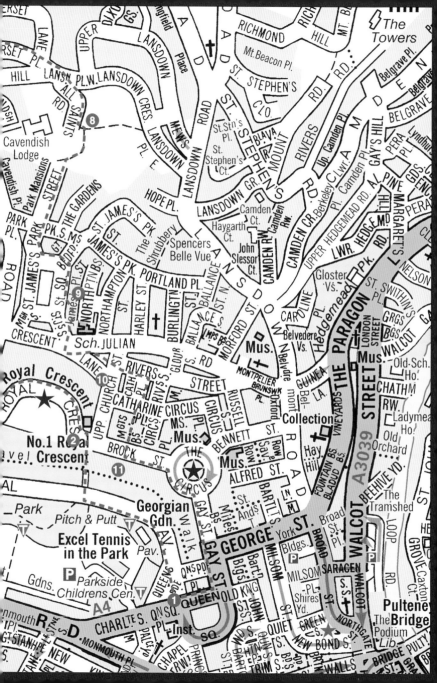

Park at Charlotte Street Car Park or any other city centre car park; or take the short walk to Queen Square from Bath Spa Station (15 minutes) or any city centre bus stop.

**1** From the northwest (top left) corner of Queen Square, walk uphill along Queens Parade. Passing the war memorial, proceed through the elaborate gates and climb Royal Avenue. At the highest point of the road, turn right up a footpath to reach the Royal Crescent ★ .

**2** Take a walk around the crescent and then descend Marlborough Buildings to return to the end of Royal Avenue. Turn right into Royal Victoria Park ★ . Follow the road until you reach the ponds on the right. Thread your way through the ponds, eventually returning to the road.

**3** When the road turns up the hill, take the parallel footpath to the right of it. This will lead you to the Botanical Gardens ★ . Explore the Botanical Gardens at your leisure, eventually leaving via the gate above the ornamental pond.

**4** If you're wearing suitable footwear, cross the park road and go through another gate to enter the Great Dell ★ , a hilly glade of cypress and sequoia trees. Head to the right to follow a pleasant path around the perimeter of the Dell. Returning to the park road through the same gate, set off up the hill, taking the footpath on the left-hand side of the road.

**5** When the park road comes out on Weston Road, cross Weston Road and take the footpath on the far side (left fork), signed as the Cotswold Way. The path climbs up through the Bath Approach Golf Course. A good view over the Avon Valley opens out to the left as you climb.

**6** Emerging on quiet Sion Hill, turn right and climb past the houses. Turn right at the top of the hill to walk along the flat section of Sion Hill; after a while you will start to descend again.

**7** Cross the top end of Cavendish Road, go straight on and then climb the steps on the left to reach the graceful crescent of Somerset Place. Coming out on Lansdown Place West, go straight on for a short distance and then bear right down All Saints Road.

**8** Take the footpath to the left of the last cottage and then follow it down past the side of the cottage, coming out on Park Street. Proceed steeply downhill until you reach St James's Square. Turn left to walk around the garden square in a clockwise direction.

**9** Just before you reach the bottom corner of the square, turn left through an archway to reach St James's Place. Carry on down to come out on St James's Street. At the bottom of St James's Street, turn left onto Julian Road to reach a triangular green space at Crescent Lane.

**10** Make your way to the far side of the green and cross Upper Church Street into Rivers Street, then take the second right so you descend the far side of Catharine Place. Go straight on into pedestrianized Margaret's Buildings and continue to the end.

**11** Turn left into Brock Street to reach the unique residential layout of The Circus ★. Take the first right out of The Circus, Gay Street, to return to Queen Square.

# **AZ** walk sixteen

## The Height of Grandeur

Bath's highest Georgian terraces on Lansdown hill.

Bath nestles in the Avon valley on the edge of the Cotswolds, and the city is surrounded by hills. One such hill is Lansdown, a steep escarpment to the north of the city. Bath's Georgian and Regency era development spread up the slopes of Lansdown as the developers of prestigious residential terraces sought to make the best of the city views. Even further up the hill, a number of exclusive educational establishments were founded.

You will need strong legs to tackle this walk, which begins at Queen Square in the city centre before climbing steeply up through the back streets of Lansdown hill, passing the historic Assembly Rooms on the way. Eventually you will reach the elegant, view-commanding Lansdown Crescent and Somerset Place.

You will then proceed to the secluded Sion Hill Place, the highest of Bath's formal terraces, before climbing further still to do a circuit of leafy College Road.

Passing the landscaped grounds of the exclusive Kingswood Preparatory School and the Royal High School, you will descend via quiet streets and footpaths with city and country views to reach the laid-back green space of Hedgemead Park before returning to Queen Square.

| | |
|---|---|
| **start / finish** | Queen Square, Bath |
| **nearest postcode** | BA1 2HX |
| **distance** | 3¾ miles / 6 km |
| **time** | 2 hours |
| **terrain** | All surfaced roads and paths, some steps. The first half of the walk is a steep and largely continuous climb. |

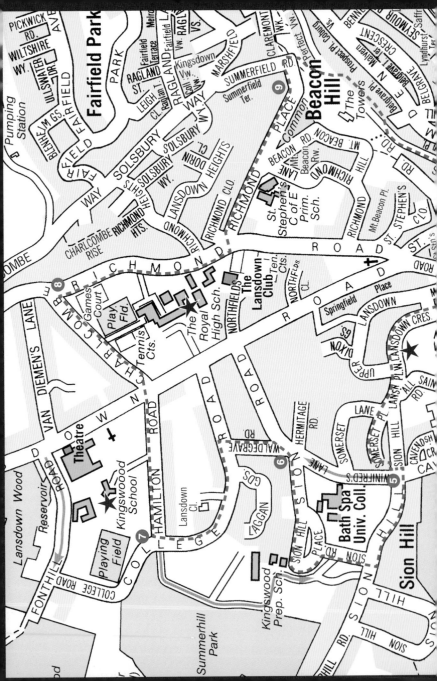

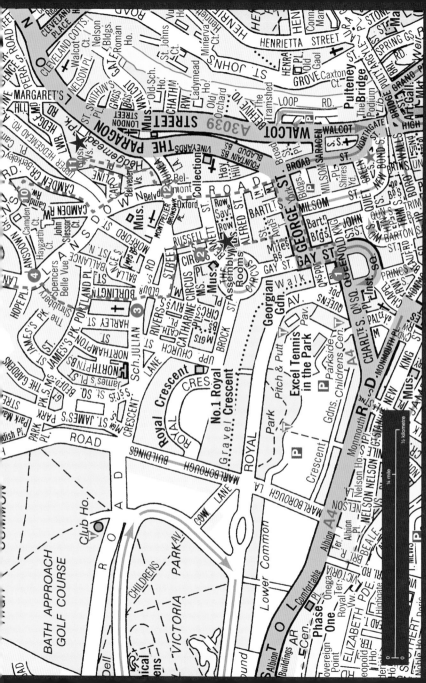

Park at Charlotte Street Car Park or any other city centre car park; or take the short walk to Queen Square from Bath Spa Station (15 minutes) or any city centre bus stop.

**1** From the top right (northeast) corner of Queen Square, climb Gay Street, keeping to the left. At George Street turn right, crossing over to the upper side of the road and walking with the railings on your right. Turn left along quiet Miles's Buildings, turning left again after the corner to reach the Assembly Rooms ★, which were built in the 18th century as a venue for all manner of social gatherings and quickly became a hub for high Bath society. Climb up past the Assembly Rooms and turn right along Bennett Street.

**2** Immediately turn left up Russell Street to reach Rivers Street, giving you a view of Christ Church to the right. Turn left into Rivers Street and then right into Gloucester Street to reach Julian Road.

**3** Cross Julian Road and climb Burlington Street opposite, passing St Mary's Catholic Church. Bear left into grand Portland Place then, just before you start passing smaller houses, turn right and climb The Shrubbery, a steep footpath that will lead you to Lansdown Road.

**4** Turn left and climb Lansdown Road for a short distance, where you will have a view of St Stephen's Church further up the hill. Take the left turn into Lansdown Place East to reach the elegant Lansdown Crescent ★. As you walk around the grand crescent, enjoy the city views to the left. Continue down Lansdown Place West and then bear right into the exclusive Somerset Place. Descend the steps opposite the far end of the terrace to return to the road.

**5** Crossing the top of Cavendish Road, climb steep Sion Hill to find yourself among quiet Georgian villas. Turn right through a set of stone gateposts to reach Sion Road, which climbs past the leafy Sion Hill campus of Bath Spa University. Bear left at the top of the straight section to reach the secluded Regency-era enclave of Sion Hill Place, and then rejoin Sion Road.

**6** At the top of Winifred's Lane, bear left briefly and then turn left to climb Waldegrave Road, an unmade private road that leads into an exclusive neighbourhood of large, detached houses. Turn left to make a circuit of College Road as you finally climb to the highest point on our walk.

**7** At the next junction, turn right along the dead straight Hamilton Road. You will pass the landscaped grounds of the exclusive Kingswood Preparatory School ★ on the left, eventually returning to Lansdown Road. Cross the main road carefully and go straight on along Charlcombe Lane, where you will glimpse views of the countryside as you finally begin to descend.

**8** At the next junction, turn right onto Richmond Road. The road skirts the historic campus of the Royal High School ★. Further countryside views can be glimpsed between the properties on the left. Reaching a fork, bear left into Richmond Place, following the historic terrace to the far end.

**9** Eventually, Richmond Place becomes Summerfield Road. Continue to the first corner and then turn right down a flight of steps. Immediately turn right again to descend a steep woodland footpath. Reaching the end of a secluded terrace called Perfect View, turn right onto a pleasant footpath. The path merges with the driveway to a grand property before coming out at a hairpin bend on St Stephen's Road. Take the high road to see a great view over the rooftops on the left.

**10** When St Stephen's Road starts to climb again, turn left down a flight of steps to reach the lower part of the road. Descend the hill and then bear right to reach Camden Crescent, another grand Georgian terrace that benefits from views out over the valley. Coming back out on Lansdown Road (here also called Bellevue), turn left past a couple of shops and then turn left again into Caroline Place. Descending past a quiet terrace, the mews ends at a footpath.

**11** Turn right down the path and immediately right again to enter peaceful Hedgemead Park ★. Follow the footpath around the top of the park until you return to Lansdown Road.

**12** Cross Lansdown Road and then make your way back down to George Street. Turn right into George Street (here also called York Buildings). Crossing over at the traffic lights just before Milsom Street, go straight on to return to Gay Street and then turn left to return to Queen Square.

# ᴀZ walk seventeen

## Railways and Tunnels

Historical lines southwest of Bath city centre.

The southwest part of Bath is home to a large sprawl of pleasant Victorian housing. Centred around Oldfield Park, the area feels quite separate from the Georgian city centre thanks to the double barrier of the River Avon and the Great Western Railway. The area is also home to the Two Tunnels Greenway, a stretch of the former Somerset & Dorset Joint Railway that has been converted to a shared pedestrian and cycle path.

Starting at Bath Spa Station, this walk takes a meandering route out through residential Oldfield Park. Strong walkers can opt to make the strenuous climb up Beechen Cliff to the viewpoint at Alexandra Park, which offers spectacular city views.

Not far beyond Oldfield Park Station the route joins the Two Tunnels Greenway, which is a pleasant wildlife corridor as well as a foot and cycle path, climbing gradually up to the 447-yard (409-metre) Devonshire Tunnel. After a stroll through the cool gloom of the tunnel, the walk descends into leafy Lyncombe Vale for a taste of the countryside within the city. You have the option to take a detour to the iconic mile-long (1.6-km) Combe Down Tunnel before making one last climb.

A long descent via Lyncombe Hill will return you to Bath Spa Station and the attractions of the city centre.

| | |
|---|---|
| **start / finish** | Brunel Square, Dorchester Street, Bath |
| **nearest postcode** | BA1 1SX |
| **distance** | 4¼ miles / 6.9 km |
| **time** | 2 hours 15 minutes |
| **terrain** | Mostly surfaced roads and paths with a short unsurfaced section, some steps. Optional steep climb. |

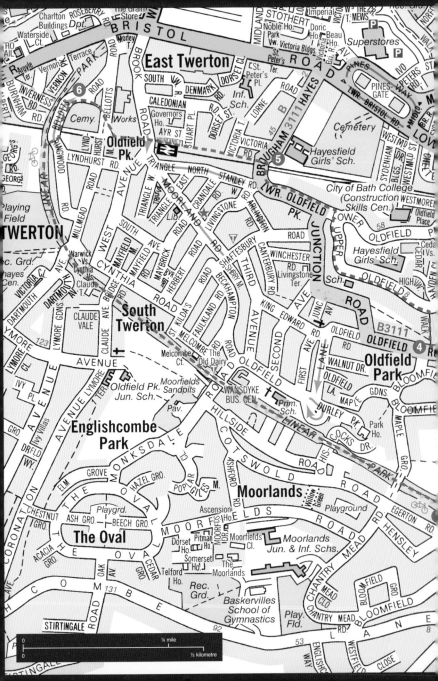

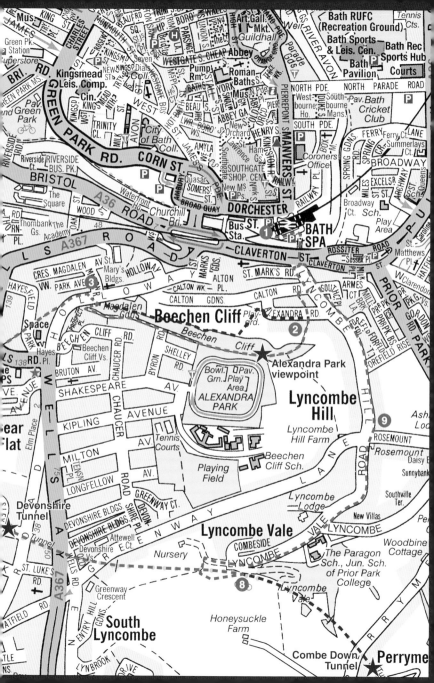

The walk starts outside Bath Spa railway station. Parking is available at nearby Avon Street Car Park and other city centre car parks. Alternatively, you can take any bus to Dorchester Street or Bath Bus Station.

**1** Starting in Brunel Square outside the railway station, surrounded by bars and restaurants, begin by taking the pedestrian tunnel under the railway lines. Cross the little car park at the back of the station and then turn right across the Halfpenny Bridge. Cross both arms of Claverton Street at the traffic lights, turning right for a short distance and then left into Lyncombe Hill. After a short climb, turn right into Calton Road then immediately left onto a narrow footpath. Climb up to Alexandra Road.

**2** There are two options at this point. Strong walkers should continue up the footpath, making the steep and strenuous climb to Alexandra Park ★ , which offers spectacular views of the city; follow the path along the bottom edge of the park and then below the houses beyond, eventually heading back downhill to come out on Holloway. Alternatively, for a more level walk, turn right along Alexandra Road; at the bend, take the footpath ahead of you and then turn left to follow a winding path through Beechen Cliff woods, rejoining the main route when the path comes out on Holloway.

**3** Cross Holloway to reach the raised pavement and then turn left up the hill. After a short distance, climb a broad flight of stone steps on the right to reach a pleasant footpath between the houses. Go straight across Hayesfield Park and continue to the busy Wells Road. Very carefully, cross the road; there is limited visibility next to the footpath, so find a safer spot elsewhere on the bend. Go straight on into Oldfield Road.

**4** Turn right after the bus stop onto a footpath going down the hill. Ignore the footpath that turns off to the left and continue down to Upper Oldfield Park. Turn left and follow the winding street down past Hayesfield School. At the end of the road, cross Lower Oldfield Park and turn left. Follow the main road round to the right until you have crossed the railway tracks.

**5** Turn left along a path next to the railway line. You will pass terraced houses and Oldfield Park Station. Reaching Brook Road, cross to another footpath. Follow it past industrial buildings and go straight on so that you skirt Twerton Cemetery. You will come out on Bellotts Road outside the cemetery gates.

**6** Continue round the outside of the cemetery until you have crossed the railway tracks again, then bear right to join the Two Tunnels Greenway. Following the cycle path uphill for just under a mile (about 1.5 km), passing a variety of green spaces and occasional city views, you will eventually come to the mouth of the Devonshire Tunnel ★ .

**7** Walk through the dimly lit tunnel, allowing your eyes a few moments to adjust to the gloom. After 447 yards (409 metres) you will emerge among the pleasant woodlands of Lyncombe Vale. Continue along the cycle path until you have crossed a small bridge with low brick walls to either side.

**8** If you'd like to extend the walk, continue along the path to explore the mile-long (1.6-km) Combe Down Tunnel ★ , which has an installation of coloured lights and music at around the halfway point. Retrace your steps afterwards to rejoin the route. If you do not wish to extend the walk, or once you have visited Combe Down Tunnel and retraced your steps, leave the cycle path at this point via an earthen path on the right, which doubles back beside the cycle path. Go under the bridge that you crossed a few moments ago to reach the end of Lyncombe Vale Road. Follow the quiet road past rural properties until you reach a fork. Take the left fork to continue up Lyncombe Vale Road.

**9** At a crossroads with Greenway Lane and Rosemount Lane, go straight on to descend historic Lyncombe Hill. Reaching Claverton Street, retrace your steps over the bridge and under the railway lines to return to Bath Spa Station.

# ᴀ̶z walk eighteen

## The Village within the City

A stroll around Widcombe.

The historic village of Widcombe has long since been absorbed by the city of Bath, but it still retains its own identity today thanks to its location south of the River Avon and Kennet & Avon Canal.

This walk explores the different facets of the area, starting with the high street at the heart of the present-day Widcombe neighbourhood. From there, the route takes a pleasant stroll up the lower section of the Kennet & Avon Canal, passing a multitude of lock gates.

Reaching Bathwick Hill, the route turns back along graceful Sydney Buildings on its way to Widcombe Hill, from which it descends through the old village centre, passing the church and manor house.

Upon reaching Prior Park Road, an optional detour takes walkers uphill to visit the National Trust's lovely Prior Park Landscape Garden. Walkers including this detour on their journey should allow an additional half hour for the walk itself and at least an hour to explore the gardens.

The walk concludes with an optional climb up steep Rosemount Lane to return to Bath Spa Station via Lyncombe Hill.

| | |
|---|---|
| **start / finish** | Brunel Square, Dorchester Street, Bath |
| **nearest postcode** | BA1 1SX |
| **distance** | 2½ miles / 4 km (+ optional 1 mile / 1.6 km) |
| **time** | 1 hour 30 minutes (+ optional 30 minutes) |
| **terrain** | All surfaced roads and paths. Some steps and one optional steep climb. |

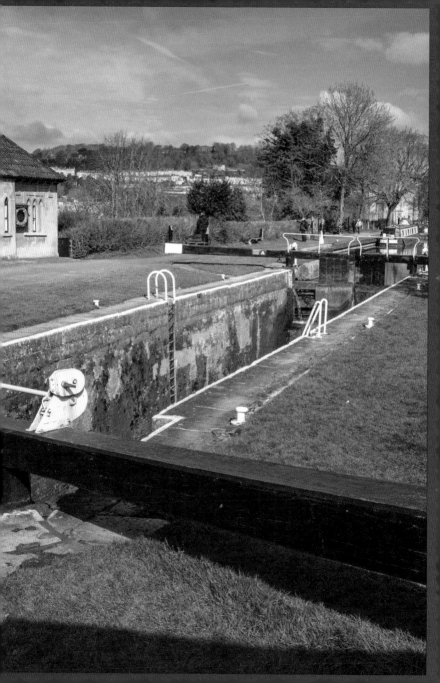

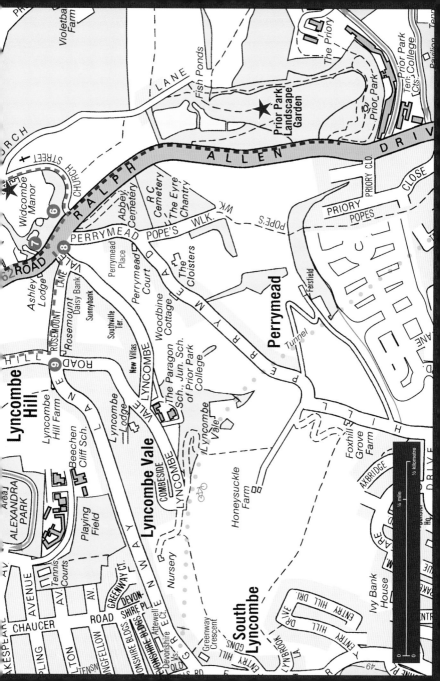

The walk starts outside Bath Spa railway station. Parking is available at nearby Avon Street Car Park and other city centre car parks. Alternatively, you can take any bus to Dorchester Street or Bath Bus Station.

**1** Starting in Brunel Square outside the railway station, surrounded by bars and restaurants, begin by taking the pedestrian tunnel under the railway lines. Cross the little car park at the back of the station and then turn right across the Halfpenny Bridge. Cross both arms of Claverton Street at the traffic lights then turn left along Claverton Buildings, entering Widcombe's pleasant high street where independent businesses predominate.

**2** At a junction of four roads, head left so that you cross the canal. Turn right onto the canal towpath and climb gradually up past a series of lock gates. You will cross one road along the way (Pulteney Gardens), before reaching an attractive section of the canal where several boats are moored. Eventually, via a short flight of steps, you will come out on Bathwick Hill next to a local supermarket.

**3** Turn right up Bathwick Hill and almost immediately right again into historic Sydney Buildings. Follow Sydney Buildings until it goes round a long right-hand bend and becomes Horseshoe Walk.

**4** When you reach a large grassy slope on the left, turn left up a tarmac footpath so you climb to the top of Abbey View. Pause to enjoy the views of the city, then go straight on, taking the right fork into The Tyning.

**5** Cross Widcombe Hill to reach Church Street. Follow Church Street round to the left to reach the heart of old Widcombe village, where you will find St Thomas' Church and the imposing Widcombe Manor ★ with its grand entrance gates. Be sure to bear right when you reach the church. You will eventually come out at the top of Prior Park Road.

**6** If you wish to visit Prior Park Landscape Garden ★ , turn left up the main road (Ralph Allen Drive) and climb it until you reach the entrance. The garden is best reached on foot as it has no car park. After your visit, retrace your steps to the junction of Prior Park Road and Church Street.

**7** The final section of the main route includes a steep climb to the top of Lyncombe Hill. If you would like to skip this section, simply turn right down Prior Park Road to return to Bath Spa Station via the main road and Widcombe high street.

**8** Otherwise, cross Prior Park Road, descend very briefly and then turn left into Lyncombe Vale. Take the first right to climb the pleasant but very steep Rosemount Lane.

**9** At a crossroads with Greenway Lane and Lyncombe Vale Road, turn right to descend historic Lyncombe Hill. Returning to Claverton Street, retrace your steps back to Bath Spa Station.

# ᴀz walk nineteen

## Valley and Views

Smallcombe valley and the Bath Skyline walk.

Bath is a small city, and there are many places where the countryside is close to town; none more so than at Smallcombe, a quiet wooded valley that is only a very short walk from the city centre.

This walk takes you out of the city to explore the Smallcombe area. Starting from the iconic Pulteney Bridge, you will follow the North Parade past Bath's two main sports grounds to join the Kennet & Avon Canal at Bathwick. From there you will climb straight up to Smallcombe valley, quickly entering rural surroundings. After passing through a secluded cemetery with two unique chapels, you will find yourself in Smallcombe Woods, where the bustle of the city seems a world away. You will need good footwear for this section.

After climbing to the top of the valley, you will follow part of the Bath Skyline walk at Widcombe Hill. This designated 6-mile (9.6-km) route has been waymarked by the National Trust and provides spectacular views of the city including Bath Abbey and Lansdown. Making your way back across the valley to Bathwick Meadow, you will make a gradual descent back into Bath through a very comfortable residential area.

For the final stretch of the walk, you will return to the city centre via the historic Sydney Gardens and Great Pulteney Street.

| | |
|---|---|
| **start / finish** | Pulteney Bridge, Bath |
| **nearest postcode** | BA2 4AX |
| **distance** | 3½ miles / 5.5 km |
| **time** | 2 hours |
| **terrain** | Some unsurfaced paths, which can be slippery and muddy after bad weather. Steep hills and steps. Suitable footwear is required. |

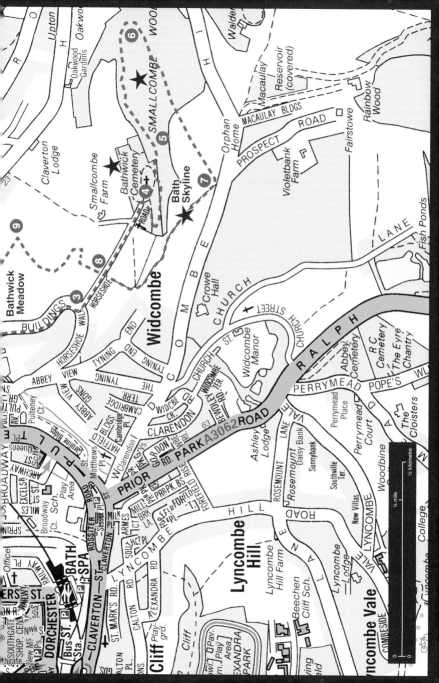

Park at Avon Street Car Park or any other city centre car park; or take the short walk to Pulteney Bridge from Bath Spa Station (10 minutes) or any city centre bus stop.

**1** From Pulteney Bridge ★ , begin by walking south along Grand Parade, passing Pulteney Weir and the Parade Gardens ★ . Turn left onto North Parade and cross North Parade Bridge, following North Parade Road past Bath Cricket Club.

**2** Cross busy Pulteney Road at the traffic lights and walk through the tunnel under the railway viaduct to reach a steep footpath. Climb up to the Kennet & Avon Canal. Turn right briefly along the towpath and then left across a little bridge, climbing up to Sydney Buildings. Turn right and follow the graceful street.

**3** On the long bend leading round to Horseshoe Walk, turn left onto a private road signed for Smallcombe Farm. Make your way along the unmade road, which quickly takes on the feel of a country lane. Eventually you will reach the entrance to the cemetery ★ , which incorporates 'the churchyard of St Mary the Virgin, Bathwick'.

**4** There are two gates: enter the cemetery via the gates on the right, approaching an unusual round chapel. Take the path that climbs up to the left of the chapel, then turn left along a path that runs just outside the treeline. After you pass through a gap in a stone wall, bear right up a path that climbs up into the trees, overlooking a second chapel. At the top of the hill, take the left fork, dipping down slightly until you reach a flight of steps on the right. Climb the steps to leave the cemetery, entering Smallcombe Woods ★ .

**5** Go straight on along a fairly well-maintained dirt path through the woods and you will find yourself shadowing the edge of a field with a stream on your left. As you leave the field behind, stay alongside the stream, following the path through fallen trees until it becomes a steep flight of steps.

**6** Eventually the steps turn away from the stream. At the top of the steps, the path splits in two. Take the right-hand route, walking along a flat path that can be muddy. Eventually you will see a brightness ahead of you as you approach a gate leading out of the woods. Go out through the gate and straight on across the open meadow beyond, so that you approach Widcombe Hill at an angle.

**7** Just before you come out on Widcombe Hill, turn right through a gate into another meadow. You are now on the Bath Skyline walk ★, and you will see the city spread out below you. Follow the well-trodden path through the meadow, descending to a gap in the hedge line. Going through another gate, go straight down the next field to return to the private road you walked along earlier.

**8** Cross the road and go through the gate opposite, to climb the footpath beyond. Cross the next field, making for a gap in the hedge on the far side.

**9** Go through the gap and then turn left along the hedge line, following the trodden path to reach Bathwick Meadow ★. Going through a gap in another hedge, the path forks. Bear right to stay on the high ground and exit onto Bathwick Hill.

**10** Carefully cross Bathwick Hill and go straight on along Cleveland Walk. Eventually, turn left down Sham Castle Lane. Bear right at the bottom of the hill, overlooking the canal, to reach Sydney Road.

**11** Carefully cross Sydney Road and go through the park gate opposite to reach Sydney Gardens ★. Cross the canal via the first footbridge, bear left and then cross the railway line. Follow the tarmac path down the left-hand side of the gardens to come out on Sydney Place.

**12** Turn right along Sydney Place, passing the Holburne Museum ★. Cross the main road at the traffic lights and take Great Pulteney Street opposite the museum. Follow Great Pulteney Street to return to Pulteney Bridge.

# AZ walk twenty

## A Georgian Folly

Sham Castle and the Kennet & Avon Canal.

Where Bristol has Blaise Castle, Bath has Sham Castle. The two have much in common: both are hilltop follies on the outskirts of their respective cities, built by wealthy landowners to a fortified design inspired by the stone keeps of old.

This walk includes a visit to the 18th-century Sham Castle. After a stroll down Great Pultney Street and a visit to Sydney Gardens, you will climb straight up to the castle by a direct and fairly demanding route. On the way up, you can pause to enjoy long-distance views over the city. From Sham Castle, the route makes a gradual descent through a large belt of wild woodland on its way down to the village of Bathampton. You will need good footwear for this part of the walk, which includes steep sections and is often muddy.

Crossing the main Warminster Road, the walk descends into Bathampton via its pleasant and historic high street before reaching an old stone bridge over the Kennet & Avon Canal. A quiet stroll back into Bath along the canal will allow you to admire the houseboats as you pass through a gentle section of the Avon valley and glimpse further city views. Returning to the city centre, the walk concludes with a pleasant stroll through the relaxing environs of Henrietta Park on the way back to Pulteney Bridge.

| | |
|---|---|
| start / finish | Pulteney Bridge, Bath |
| nearest postcode | BA2 4AX |
| distance | 4½ miles / 7.4 km |
| time | 2 hours 30 minutes |
| terrain | Some unsurfaced paths, which can be slippery and muddy after bad weather. Steep hills and steps. Suitable footwear is required. |

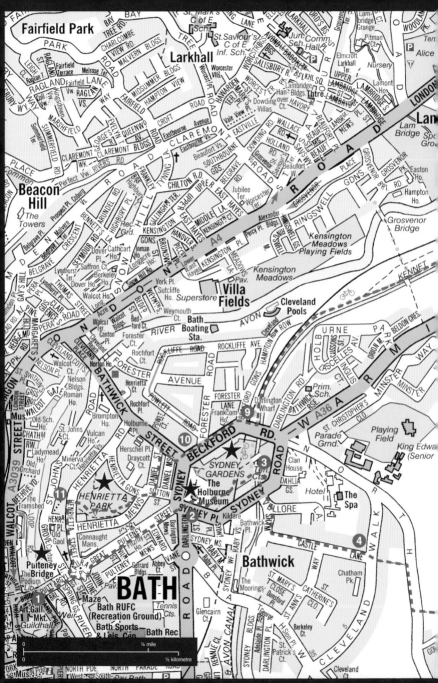

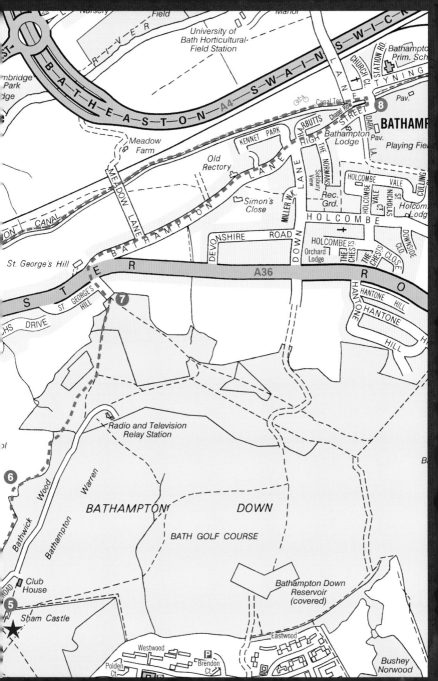

Park at Avon Street Car Park or any other city centre car park; or take the short walk to Pulteney Bridge from Bath Spa Station (10 minutes) or any city centre bus stop.

**1** Start by crossing Pulteney Bridge ★, away from the city centre, and making your way down the grand Great Pulteney Street towards the Holburne Museum ★.

**2** Cross the main road and head to the right of the Holburne Museum so you start up Sydney Place. After you have passed the museum, take the first gate on the left into Sydney Gardens ★. Sticking to the tarmac paths, make your way around the right-hand side of the gardens so that you cross the railway line and then the Kennet & Avon Canal.

**3** After you have crossed the canal, turn right and go out through the gate onto Sydney Road. Carefully cross Sydney Road and take the turning for Sham Castle Lane just above the canal. Follow Sham Castle Lane round a corner and then steadily uphill through a quiet residential area until the road ends at Cleveland Walk.

**4** Pause for breath and check out the view, then cross Cleveland Walk and continue up a footpath. Turn right up North Road until you see a gate leading to another footpath opposite. Carefully cross North Road, go through the gate and climb the steps until you come out at a viewpoint on Golf Course Road.

**5** First take a detour to see Sham Castle ★ itself. Cross Golf Course Road and take a dirt path which, after a short additional climb, will take you straight to the folly. The folly was built in the late 18th century for the local entrepreneur Ralph Allen, supposedly to improve the view from his townhouse in Bath. Afterwards, retrace your steps to the viewpoint on Golf Course Road. With the view of Bath spread out below you, take the footpath that heads off into the woods on the right. The first section is signed as the Bath Skyline walk. Be warned that the ground is very uneven and can be muddy.

**6** After a short while, you will reach a pedestrian gate where a path comes up from the left. Do not go through the gate. Instead, bear right slightly and then go straight on so that you walk with the fence to your left, quickly leaving the Bath Skyline walk. The next section covers nearly half a mile (650 metres). Continue going straight on through the woods, ignoring all side turnings. Eventually, you will begin to descend. The descent is steep at times and the ground can be slippery and muddy, so tread carefully.

**7** You will come out of the woods next to a gate on the left that leads to a gravel track. Go through the gate and make your way down to the main A36 Warminster Road. Very carefully cross the busy road and take Bathampton Lane, opposite, so that you descend gradually into the heart of Bathampton village.

**8** Bathampton Lane eventually becomes the village High Street and will bring you to an old stone bridge over the Kennet & Avon Canal. Cross the bridge and then join the canal towpath, heading to the left as seen from the bridge. Watch out for cyclists, as the towpath is part of the National Cycle Network. Follow the towpath back into Bath.

**9** After walking along the towpath for nearly 1½ miles (about 2 km), you will see that you are about to pass back under the A36, here called Beckford Road. Bear right instead so that you come out on the road. Turn right, crossing the railway line and descending towards the city centre.

**10** At the bottom of the hill, turn right into Bathwick Street and then left into Daniel Street. At the end of the road, turn right, enter Henrietta Park ★ via the corner gate and follow the footpath along the left-hand edge of the park.

**11** You will come out on Henrietta Street. Turn left along Henrietta Street and then right along Argyle Street to return to Pulteney Bridge.

# images